CAMBRIDGE LIBRARY COLLECTION

Books of enduring scholarly value

Education

This series focuses on educational theory and practice, particularly in the context of eighteenth- and nineteenth-century Europe and its colonies, and America. During this period, the questions of who should be educated, to what age, to what standard and using what curriculum, were widely debated. The reform of schools and universities, the drive towards improving women's education, and the movement for free (or at least low-cost) schools for the poor were all major concerns both for governments and for society at large. The books selected for reissue in this series discuss key issues of their time, including the 'appropriate' levels of instruction for the children of the working classes, the emergence of adult education movements, and proposals for the higher education of women. They also cover topics that still resonate today, such as the nature of education, the role of universities in the diffusion of knowledge, and the involvement of religious groups in establishing and running schools.

Labour and Childhood

Celebrated for her pioneering work to improve the education, health and welfare of slum children, Margaret McMillan (1860–1931) was an active socialist campaigner and member of the Independent Labour Party. Her involvement with Bradford school boards drew her attention to the poor state of health of the pupils – rickets, scurvy, anaemia and malnutrition were commonplace. Working with her sister Rachel (1859–1917), as well as lobbying for improved standards, Margaret opened the country's first school clinic in Bow in 1908. The sisters' most famous enterprise, the Deptford Camp School, soon followed, and the Rachel McMillan College for training nurses and teachers was founded in 1930. One of her many influential books on pre-school and primary education, this work of 1907 considers the vital role of the school doctor and argues that the practice of poor schoolchildren engaging in part-time labour is detrimental to their well-being.

Cambridge University Press has long been a pioneer in the reissuing of out-of-print titles from its own backlist, producing digital reprints of books that are still sought after by scholars and students but could not be reprinted economically using traditional technology. The Cambridge Library Collection extends this activity to a wider range of books which are still of importance to researchers and professionals, either for the source material they contain, or as landmarks in the history of their academic discipline.

Drawing from the world-renowned collections in the Cambridge University Library and other partner libraries, and guided by the advice of experts in each subject area, Cambridge University Press is using state-of-the-art scanning machines in its own Printing House to capture the content of each book selected for inclusion. The files are processed to give a consistently clear, crisp image, and the books finished to the high quality standard for which the Press is recognised around the world. The latest print-on-demand technology ensures that the books will remain available indefinitely, and that orders for single or multiple copies can quickly be supplied.

The Cambridge Library Collection brings back to life books of enduring scholarly value (including out-of-copyright works originally issued by other publishers) across a wide range of disciplines in the humanities and social sciences and in science and technology.

Labour and Childhood

M ARGARET M C M ILLAN

CAMBRIDGE
UNIVERSITY PRESS

CAMBRIDGE
UNIVERSITY PRESS

University Printing House, Cambridge, CB2 8BS, United Kingdom

Published in the United States of America by Cambridge University Press, New York

Cambridge University Press is part of the University of Cambridge.
It furthers the University's mission by disseminating knowledge in the pursuit of
education, learning and research at the highest international levels of excellence.

www.cambridge.org
Information on this title: www.cambridge.org/9781108062411

© in this compilation Cambridge University Press 2013

This edition first published 1907
This digitally printed version 2013

ISBN 978-1-108-06241-1 Paperback

LABOUR AND CHILDHOOD

LABOUR
AND CHILDHOOD

"THE KINGDOM OF HEAVEN IS WITHIN YOU."

BY

MARGARET McMILLAN

AUTHOR OF "EARLY CHILDHOOD" AND "EDUCATION THROUGH
THE IMAGINATION," ETC.

LONDON
SWAN SONNENSCHEIN & CO., Ltd.
25 HIGH STREET, BLOOMSBURY
1907

TO THE MEMORY OF MY GRANDFATHER
WHO WAS AS A FATHER TO ME
AND WHOSE GENTLE AND CHIVALROUS CHARACTER
FIRST TAUGHT ME TO HAVE FAITH
IN HUMANITY

CONTENTS

INTRODUCTORY

NO one will deny that we are living in a period of great social upheaval and unrest. A great thrill has passed through this country—a thrill of wonder, of mingled joy and alarm, and in some quarters perhaps of terror. The old political parties no longer face each other in the field, alone. *Another* is between them, who looks at each, but gives allegiance to neither. The masses have awakened, as it seems, suddenly. And it is pretty certain that they will look at every great question of human interest from a new standpoint and with a new aim.

There is no vista on which the light strikes more strangely for the newly-opened eyes than on that covered by the word Education. A little while ago there was nothing that could be called education for the masses in England. And even in recent days education has meant for the labouring man a wrangle between the sects : a quarrel for religious supremacy —and the three R's! But the morning light is even now tearing aside the shadows of ecclesiastical authority, and in the ear of Demos a fresh cry rings, fresh and new as from the lips of Morning: " What is Man ? And what can you make of him ? "

What can you make of him, toiler and bearer of burdens, you the unlearned, who have been called the last? It is an old question, but it has to be answered in a new fashion. Here tradition will not serve. To follow the path of mere tradition now would be, for the masses, to wipe out all the glory of their own advent. Is there anything in their experience which can supply them with a new answer to this old question, and which can also give them faith and courage to work for the realization of a new ideal? If not, then their new political power itself will in the end only prove a snare to them. They will be baffled by the same forces which in the past have proved too great for them. The spell which kept them half-conscious bearers of burdens, and which threatens still to keep them mere parts of a great machine driven by a power that ignores them, will still work.

But the working classes and their representatives may have a new word to speak on education. In any case, their experience furnishes ample materials for such a new message. Not forty years have passed

since the three R's began to be taught to the masses
by law! Are they, then, more learned than the
scholars and leisured class? No, indeed. But it is
a mistake to think that books contain the only
record of humanity. If all the books in the world
were burned to-morrow, the record of the race would
still be written in *the tools that have been made.*
There is, it would appear, a prophecy in work. There
are museums where the tools are ranged in order
like the letters of an alphabet. But they are not an
alphabet. Each of them is a word—a sentence
rather—and they tell a story. They throw a strange
light on the doings of their makers. An awful
method begins to reveal itself now even in the seem-
ing madness of the people—and the tools reveal this
method. It was the human hand that worked out
language, just as it was the hand that first made
tools. And the tools themselves are a language—a
kind of literature.

To the hand labourer, and to the school doctor,
much reference is made in this book. At the first
blush it may seem that they have nothing to do with
one another—that the artizan or hand labourer and
the school doctor are far apart, and that neither
have much to do with education! Well, this book
is nothing more or less than an attempt to show

that though these two men—artizan and doctor or physiologist—have long walked apart, yet one is always following the other; that on these two depended human progress, and that there can be no great advance in education till their relation to one another is understood in schools and the function of each represented more or less by those who have to prepare the youth of any generation for their life-work.

It is disease and the fear of infection and racial decline that (more than anything else, perhaps) makes us now turn to the school doctor. The fear of infection is growing acute because we have learned more about its dangers, and also because, having drawn the children of the masses into schools—that is to say, gathered together and exposed those who are the most susceptible of all—we are alarmed by the possible consequences. Our fears are well grounded, and there is no doubt that the *immediate* duty of the school doctor is to minimize the risks of school attendance. But beyond all this there are new duties awaiting him. His *real* work does not consist in the mere dealing with questions of sanitation and the prevention of infection any more than does the real work of the musician consist in the tuning of instruments. His real work is concerned with the healthy organism. His goal is education—not the mere checking of disease or infection.

The teacher's power and influence are not threatened by this new advent. They are safeguarded. The new light brought in by the school doctor must deliver the teacher from much ignorant tyranny and misrepresentation. It will free him from the torture of striving to do impossible things. Hitherto there have been inspectors and examiners of method, but there was no one to say at the right moment, " Do not insist—It is torture" or " Do not persist—It is folly." Barriers invisible to the mere " classical master" existed, and the teacher often had to fling himself against these in vain. But there is a kind of knowledge which the school doctor is always winning, and which makes clear to him what the teacher's task is.[1]

---

[1] This does not dethrone the teacher. The " rôle" of either is different from that of the other, and the kind of knowledge each has acquired is different, and also complementary. A curious example of the *naïveté* of great physicians was offered the other day to a very humble teacher. " When I think of the people's children," he said to her, " I always think of my own little girl. I would like every girl child to play just as I see *her* play. Now, I notice how she teaches herself hygiene. She plays with her doll. She undresses it, washes it all over every night and morning. She brushes its hair, washes its teeth, looks at its nails (it has none, but that is no matter). Well, this play is capital. I should have all the little girls in school taught to

This little book is nothing but a study of the
original contributions made to education by the
handworkers and mechanics of the race.   For a long
time the relation between these doers and thinkers
was never fairly realized or accepted.   They stood
apart.   They seem to stand apart still.   The tool
and the man were separated.   Sometimes the tool
was worshipped, while the man who made it was
despised as a slave.   There were magic swords, like
King Arthur's, made by nameless workers.   And yet
the study of the human organism was attempted.
"Know thyself," cried the great Greek; and the
thinkers strove to know themselves.

    They strove very honestly.   All the great religions
are founded in hygiene.   But the contempt for hand

prepare themselves in the same way for motherhood.   My child does it
voluntarily, but others could be taught such plays."
    The teacher could not help smiling.   Certainly our great doctors
have something to learn, as well as a world of things to teach in our
schools.   Play, as the teacher knew to her cost, is a living through of
something that has been already experienced.   It deals *with memories.*
The doctor's little daughter played what she knew, and it was her *own*
play.   But to impose this mere skeleton of real play on poor children who
have never known a morning bath and have never used a hair or tooth
brush—what a mockery !   The "play" is merely a new task.   The
teacher knew this very well.   She had taken no degrees, and had no
knowledge of medicine.   But she had had the opportunity of observing
the children of the poor, and so she knew that this new play would not
even amuse her children, still less make them love the bath or the
toothbrush !

labour and the slave made rapid progress impossible. Beautiful work was done by all manner of bondsmen, of helots, of serfs, and villeins; but the "scholars" turned away from the study of such people and their work. To be sure, *all* did not turn away completely. The ethical teachers found their impetus in the study of the body. Thus Plato in youth was a sculptor, and Aristotle the son and grandson of physicians. Coming down the centuries, we find the *life*-sciences, even in their crudest, rudest forms, still giving their impetus to the pioneer. From Paracelsus, with his perplexities, to clearer thinkers, such as Harvey, Galileo, Priestley, Galvani, Lavoisier. Even in our generation the same influences determine the bent of genius. Darwin was a doctor's son, and Herbert Spencer a student of physiology, and more especially of the nervous system.

But the two factors in the whole problem—that is to say, the worker and his tools—were not often studied together. Their relation to one another was as a rule ignored even by great writers. And so there were theories of education, but no science. And neither workman nor physiologist, save those by chance admitted, darkened the doors of the modern elementary schools until, in very recent days, a movement was begun to admit at least the latter.

And now at last Disease is driving the doctor into schools! Disease and failure![1] A kind of failure that is, however, not nearly so new as we imagine; for it always appears when the workman is banished. There is a kind of stupidity that was noted long ago by Luther, and named by learned men "*Stupor Scholasticus.*" Luther declared that "boys got this particular kind of stupidity from sitting much in schools." Perhaps men get it, too, from sitting too much apart in very high places — from taking no part, however small, in the rougher kind of manual labour. But where the worker and inventor comes, this particular kind of dullness vanishes.

The generation that determines to get real education will banish it for ever. But it cannot be banished without the introduction of manual work into schools. Nor can it be banished without the help of the physiologist.

.   .   .   .

Every difficulty that a teacher encounters begins and ends with the organism of the child. There is the power. There too is the defect or weakness.

---

[1] In speaking of failure, I do not cast any shadow on the fair work achieved by thousands of good teachers all over the country. I mean to imply simply that the method that excluded the physiologist and passed by the worker gave a false result—as it was bound to do.

If any subject does not invoke power and improve health it is not worth learning. But nearly all school subjects may do this. To take the common R's and writing : to learn these in the right way is as healthy an exercise as skipping or running. It is to exercise the lungs, the lips, the vocal organs, the eyes, the hands, and arms aright. It is to discover (if there be anything wrong) the risk or mischief, and be warned. Health is a by-product of right learning, and good teaching is founded on physiology.

There is, then, a Hygiene of Instruction, and to develop it as a science will be the ultimate task of the school doctor.

This little book attempts a threefold task. Its first aim is to make clear what the *immediate* task of the school doctor is.

Its second to show the trend of the only continuous education the race has received (that is to say, the trend of education through work and experience).

And last of all, having a glimpse of what has been done by the artizan, and what is being attempted already by the school doctor in this and other lands, we shall try to indicate the probable line of advance.

LABOUR AND CHILDHOOD

CHAPTER I

DISEASES AND THEIR CAUSES

THE first, the most obvious reason why the doctor is wanted to-day in schools is because a great many children are *ill*. Let us briefly run over a few facts and figures collected very recently.

A few years ago a Royal Commission was appointed to inquire into the condition of school children. The evidence then gathered was very disquieting. In Edinburgh one school doctor found 700 cases of neglected, and even unrecognized phthisis. (Dr. Leslie Mackenzie found in one slum school two children with acute phthisis, doing the ordinary school drill with the others!) In Edinburgh, 1300 of the children attending school had heart disease, and there were 15,000 cases of throat disease! The school-doctors of London have given evidence of the same kind. Dr. Thomas reports that 8 per cent of the non-wage-earning children are deformed, and that 8

B

per cent have heart disease, while 25 per cent of all the children are anæmic. Among the wage-earning children matters are much worse. From 20 to 30 per cent are backward or dull from causes that are altogether physical in the ordinary sense.

Diseases vary in different countries—just as human types, and even animals and plants, vary. The East has its own plagues. And there are no two Western countries that have exactly the same ways of getting ill and unfit. The alien brings with him his own disease—as, for example, the disease known as *favus* which exists in London, but not among English-born children, save in the case of a few who have caught the infection from foreign children. On the other hand, England has her own scourges—phthisis, for example, which still carries off young and old in great numbers. Then among school-going children there is the very common ailment called adenoids. In Scotland and in England the number of these is legion. In some quarters of Scottish cities 25 per cent of the children suffer from the distress of blocked-up nostril and throat. The Report of the Committee on Physical Deterioration had the evidence on this point of Mr. Arthur Cheadle among others. Mr. Cheadle examined the state of the ears, throat, and nose of 1000 school children between the ages of three and sixteen in the Hanwell district school, which receives the children of the poorest class from Southwark and the City of London. Of the children examined, 341, or only 34 per cent, had normal ears and hearing, and 449, or 45 per cent, were suffering from adenoids in some form or other.

Then there are the victims of eye-disease—a great army. Some of them suffer from what is known as "blight"—a word which expresses very well the sad appearance of the tearful dim eye and its red and powdered lids! Some have what is called "pink-eye," a contagious eye disease, as is "blight." Taking the children in the standards, an average of 10 per cent have bad vision. In one of his later reports Dr. Kerr mentions about a dozen eye-diseases found in the school-children of London. Many of these need skilled medical treatment. But a great many cases yield to simple hygienic treatment.[1]

[1] More than 40 per cent of the blind lose their sight through neglect—neglect in the first week of life! This fact alone might impel us to look at first and simple causes. There are not wanting men who do this for us in so far as mere individuals working alone and without much support can do it. "Mr. Bishop Harman," says Dr. Kerr, "has paid attention to the bearing of cleanliness and social conditions on eye disease. In reporting on the condition of eyelids of over 1000 children at school, Mr. Harman has made a note of the condition of eyelids and of the hair. He points out that at the age when girls are left to themselves in the matter of cleanliness the state of the eyelids grows worse. That is to say, clean hair usually goes with healthy eyelids, and vice versa."

There is the blind group, then, in our schools.
But above them there is another section of children,
who are not blind, but whose vision is such that the
ordinary school education must injure them. These
have to be discovered and provided for; but they
cannot be discovered, treated, and provided for without medical aid.

Then there is the group of skin diseases—a for-
midable one. Dr. Leslie MacKenzie mentions nine or
ten distinct skin diseases found in our schools, and
they are, of course, nearly all very contagious. Most
of them, indeed, are passed round from one child to
its neighbour as quickly almost as flame is passed
from one dry grass-blade to another. Yet they are
all preventible, and most of them, though by no
means all, can be quickly as well as perfectly banished.

The majority of parents have a horror of them all—
or of nearly all. And the majority of children, therefore, would be safe from them did safety depend on
their home-life. But it does not depend entirely on
that, for they go to school. So a very large class
of children run grave risks at schools. Many people,
of course, will not let their children run risks. It is
certain that the bulk of the middle classes will
avoid the elementary schools until many diseases

are banished. As long as these refuse to use the schools, as it were, and choose to pay for their children's schooling elsewhere, the raising of the status of the people's schools is held back, to the sad loss of children of ALL classes. The Germans have understood this, and have taken such very energetic measures that their primary schools are safe places for all to a degree undreamed of by us. That there is no safety in mere exclusiveness the record of death and failure in the past in families of high rank amply proves. In "select" schools nothing new could be discovered—the vista was too small, and the eye of teacher and parent became indolent. (This does not apply, of course, when children are isolated or taken in small schools because of some defect that makes ordinary work impossible, and when one of the objects of the teacher is close observation.)

There is, over and above all these ailments and risks due to unhealthy conditions, a large *group* of diseases which all children are liable to, such as measles, scarlet fever, whooping cough. The first of these carries off an immense number every year; and as many children come to school even before the age of five, it is of course clear that school-going involves great risks for them. In some localities the epidemic rising from even *one* case rages in more than one class-room. And this is true of other diseases which are more dangerous, though not so common as measles (and therefore responsible for fewer deaths).

Then there are the ailments that arise from school life itself. Many of them are concerned with the nervous system. But they are not, as a rule, infectious; so we need not say anything of them here. Let us keep to the epidemics. Only a few words have we written or read, but they serve to show that the trail of disease is over the schools—that many suffer, that nearly all run grave risks.

But though the medical reports are alarming, yet they are not depressing. There is evidence to show that the evil can be fairly tackled, and the danger warded off. It appears that the heredity of the mass of the children is good in a very determined kind of way—that the human race is like clear water tumbling from a polluted spout, which rises clear, though it is stained almost from the first. Moreover, we are not on the down grade, but improving. A hundred years ago the death-rate was higher than it now is, the fit perishing with the unfit in thousands.

Having rescued Hope, then, out of the black waters of these modern medical reports, let us turn to consider the average school child. It is plain that the great majority of school children must be regarded, from the physical standpoint, as decidedly gallant little persons, who have wrestled through their infancy and have managed to come out of tribulations that have killed a large proportion of all the children of their birth-years. At least one in five of all perished before the end of his fifth year, and in many districts the dead are even more numerous. However, over three-fourths have managed to survive, and are now in school. " They at least must be strong," people would have cried long ago. But the circumstances of their early lives do not encourage us to think so. The strong baby falls a victim to disease quite as fast as the weak one in so far as the most fatal infant epidemics are concerned. And, what is more to the point, *the same causes that killed many must have certainly crippled many of the survivors. The victory of the survivor is not complete.* Indeed, when looking round the modern class-room, one is tempted to think of the refuges opened for brave soldiers who have been wounded. They—the veterans—are decorated, but they are minus a leg or an arm. The child conquerors are not decorated, and their wounds are so well hidden that even the most watchful parents often fail to perceive them—in time.

But in Dr. Kerr's Report for 1905 he puts a question, and answers it. The question is this : "Do the weakly children get killed off in infancy? and do only the strong muddle through? Or does the thing that kills one in every five have a maiming effect on those that are left?"

TABLE OF INFANT MORTALITIES

	1892	1893	1894	1895	1896
London .	154	163	143	165	161
St. Saviour's .	187	154	145	205	213
St. George's .	174	206	186	198	181
Newington .	172	176	158	201	184
Camberwell .	155	161	148	164	156
Lambeth .	135	149	133	152	136

The above table gives the number of infant deaths per thousand in the years from 1892 to 1896 in different parts of London. The physique curve, or line showing the average health of the school-going children was taken, and above it the infant death-rate for the parish where the school was situated was charted. It was found that they tallied in a very remarkable way. The children's health varied according to the year in which they were born. Thus the surviving children of 1892 (the year least fatal to infants) were the strongest and tallest for their

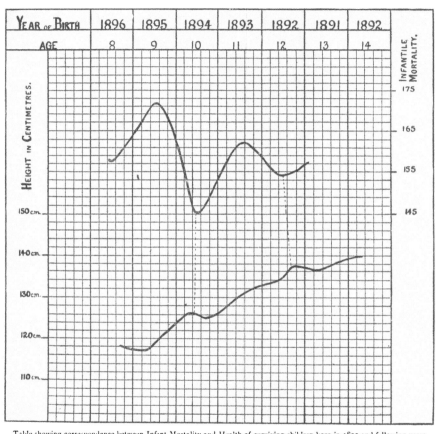

| YEAR OF BIRTH | 1896 | 1895 | 1894 | 1893 | 1892 | 1891 | 1892 |
| AGE | 8 | 9 | 10 | 11 | 12 | 13 | 14 |

Table showing correspondence between Infant Mortality and Health of surviving children born in 1892 and following years. Where Mortality line sinks, as in 1894, the Health line of children born in the same year rises.

Face page 8

age, while the survivors born in 1895 (the year of the highest death-rate of infants) were the weakest.

It would appear therefore that the children born in certain years have a harder fight for life, and that those who survive are less healthy and strong than are children born in other years. There is, however, no year that does not see a prodigious slaughter of the innocents. And there is no year, therefore, in which the children who survive are not severely handicapped through disease.

Disease, then, plays a great part in school life to-day. Not only the diseases that are infectious, but also others. Not only present diseases, but diseases that are supposed to be over and done with. And what is the effect of it all on children as learners? It appears that some kinds of disease and deformity do not hinder the development of the brain. There are few dwarfs who are inferior to other people in intelligence—not a few have been famous men—such, for example, as Æsop, and Pope. And some kinds of disease stimulate brain cells, as Dr. Kerr points out—more especially in its active stages—as, for example, when a servant girl in delirium remembers the Greek or Latin she has heard read.

Dr. Arkell, of Liverpool, points out that starvation has a strangely stimulating effect on the nervous

system of some children. Emaciated little creatures,
with skin harsh and rough, rapid pulse, nerves ever
on the strain—have yet a look of lively intelligence.
But, he adds, this is only the intelligence of a hunt-
ing animal. It is not intellect in any real sense.
The steady tendency of starvation is towards the
destruction of brain power ; disease lowers it. And
so true is this that a very large proportion of all
the children of the country, though of good race,
have become stupid merely through illness, under-
feeding, and an unhealthy mode of living.

.   .   .   .   .   .

It is hard to draw a line between the "diseased"
and those who, without being actually ill, are living
in a state of lowered vitality. If we consider the
latter to be ill, then indeed whole classes of the community must be considered ill or diseased. The
strange fact is, however, that in many cases they are
not diseased. They lose strength, intellect, power of
every kind, and yet escape disease and deformity in
a wonderful way, just as if Nature kept the door of
salvation for them open to the last.

The great cause of disease and defect is poverty—
poverty, with its sad train—overcrowding, foul air,
bad housing, insufficient or unsuitable food, worry,

overwork. These play the greatest part in fixing the death and disease rate of the country. It is because of poverty and its train that evils are created, which must be met and paid for at a heavy rate. Asylums, prisons, schools for the feeble-minded, refuges, and homes for the homeless; all these are costly. And yet they are mainly the fruits of want!

Poverty reduces some well-endowed children to the condition of creatures deprived of the upper brain.[1] In forcing children to toil it destroys the intelligence of the brilliantly endowed (at least 14 per cent of the wage-earning children of London are reckoned to be above the average *when they begin wage-earning*), and it is one of the great causes of the drink craving. For that craving betrays a primal want in the case of thousands—though not of all drinkers—the want of food. In a late number of *The Journal of Inebriety* we read that the true

---

[1] Dr. Arkell, who examined school children in Liverpool, writes: "If I told one of these (of the poorest) to open its mouth it would take no notice until the request became a command, which sometimes had to be accompanied by a slight shake to draw the child's attention. Then the mouth would be slowly opened widely, but no effort would be made to close it again until the child was told to do so. As an experiment I left one child with its mouth wide open the whole time I examined it—about four minutes—and it never once shut it. Now that shows a condition something like what one gets with a pigeon that has had its higher brain centres removed, and is a very sad thing to see in a human being."

vine is literally within us. The stimulating agents in
the blood are tiny bodies called "hormones." These
give the spur that leads to growth. These, too,
make gladness possible; they warm the chambers
of memory; they flood the consciousness with the
rosy light of hope. But if the blood is *poor*, then
the hormones languish, and the craving becomes
fierce, stimulus is wanted more than food, and it is
found in a ready-made poison. The ill-nourished
have a smaller chance of reform than those who can
eat good food, for they cannot, as it were, manu-
facture the *true* stimulant anew for themselves. Thus
the food-and-drink question are nearly always, in so
far as the poor are concerned, *two* sides of *one*
question. The closing of public-houses to children
and women is, of course, a step in the right direction.
But it is only a step, not a goal.

Then there is another cause of disease of which
school doctors did not speak for awhile, but of which
they now speak freely enough. (It is true they are
never reported, and there is still a conspiracy of
silence on the matter.) This cause is—dirt, foulness
of every description. Dr. Kerr puts it bluntly
enough. "The majority of cases of injury to health,"
he writes, "may be traced originally to a want of
cleanliness!" In one London school, which is of

course typical of many, the school doctors declared 11 per cent of the children to be "dirty and verminous," and 34 per cent "dirty in body and clothes"—that is to say 45 per cent were unfit to sit beside clean children. There were only 12 per cent of the children in this school who might be described as clean—that is to say, as clean as their neighbours would allow them to be.

But this evil, as well as others, has poverty at its *root.* "Even if one is poor, one can surely be clean!" is a common remark, but it is rather superficial. Artificial heat of every kind is costly. Hot water is not laid on in all homes—or in schools! *Cold* water appears a very cruel thing to the hungry, though pleasant to the well-nourished. Even fresh, cool air has terrors for the ill-fed. To be sure many very poor children are very clean. And a little while ago—not a hundred years ago—the children of nobles were not washed much oftener than the children of slum-dwellers. Certainly a middle-class child to-day would shrink with horror from little nobles of bygone days if these could reappear just as they were under their fine clothes! The Court of Versailles was not dainty. The ladies did not bathe, and typhoid was a common disease in palaces not very long ago. The history of Queen Anne's children shows a worse record than that of almost any slum mother to-day. But dirt is largely a result of poverty, of lack of time, strength, and money, and this was discovered by the London Education Authority when it began to look into the problem of uncleanness.

Take London, for example. The London Education Authority began by assuming that all the children had homes; and they engaged nurses to visit, not only the schools, but the homes of such children as showed signs of gross neglect. To and fro went the new servants of the Education Authority, bringing counsel and tactful works, bringing help too, where it was needed, and there is no doubt at all about the value of their work.

It was bold, however, to assume that all the children had homes. Many children live in one-room tenements. From these closely-packed chambers where they sleep, the mother, as well as children, depart, it may be, in the early morning. Of 110 boys, all very far below the average in physique, forty-four had a mother at home, but sixty-six were all practically motherless. In some cases the mother was dead, but in the rest the mother was absent all day at work.

And even in those cases where the mother was at

home, what hope was there for the children? Without any kind of wash basin or tub in the room corner, supplied by water from a yard tap used by a legion of families, with no room, no privacy, and, above all, no desire or idea of the necessity for cleanliness on the part of the parent—what prospect was offered for the child? The law, of course, *might* intervene. There is even a Cleansing of Persons Act. What in so far as children are concerned is that Act worth? Supposing that they were seized and washed by law in a specially furnished kind of bath of correction, would such measures form the basis of new habits? It is, to say the least, very unlikely. As well hope that a child could learn to love books by being forced, at rare intervals, to have a spelling lesson in a police-cell!

Some English Education Authorities have taken another line. They did not begin by engaging nurses. They did not visit homes. There was ample opportunity to judge of the home from the open street door, and the appearance of the home-keepers in the street, as well as the state of the neglected child in school. They built baths, engaged a new order of teacher. They printed leaflets, too, setting forth the need for protecting the clean child, and for making school a desirable and safe place, as well as

the duty of saving the neglected. It was prophesied
that these leaflets though carefully worded would
give offence to many. But no! They gave offence,
as it happened, to none. It was prophesied that
parental responsibility would die. But on the
contrary, parental responsibility was born in many.
In many it began for the first time to grow and
flourish apace. It was foretold that the children
who washed at school would be neglected at home.
But as time went on the children who had been
quite neglected at home began to wear cleaner
clothes, to wash (for the first time) at home so as to
come clean to the baths. What is more wonderful,
the mothers came and wanted to use the baths and
to learn swimming.

The mothers were not offended. They took to
bathing quite as naturally as did their social superiors
a generation ago. As for the prediction that parental
responsibility would be destroyed, that always was
contradicted in fact. The school experience that
brought relief to the child brought awakening to the
mothers. Parental responsibility was *created* by the
new kind of school lesson. It was born in some; it
was stimulated in many.

Last year, 1906, the Education Committee of
London beginning to feel perhaps that the prophets

were not prophesying quite truly (while medical inspection was making clear how much of all the sickness and unfitness in schools is remediable) sent their medical officer, Dr. James Kerr and the assistant educational adviser, Dr. Rose, abroad, to see and report on the school baths in Germany and Holland, and the general effect of their use on schools and children.

On their return these two travellers published a Report. In this Report they show that school baths are common abroad. Every town visited had installations for bathing children : school bathing arrangements are made, even in quite small places of three or four thousand inhabitants ! In many schools 80 per cent of all the children use the school showers, but the percentage is in some places larger, in some smaller, and there are schools such as Am Zugweg at Cologne where all the children bathe. Many of these children must of course come from good homes.

There is no need to describe all the baths visited by the London officials. Many of them are described in the Report, but we need here name only one or two.

Take for example Blucher Street School, Wiesbaden. It was built in the shining light of public

c

favour doubtless, for every school in this city has now its installation of shower baths, and no one questions the utility of this kind of class-room. Entering the playground with its pollarded trees, one passes into a school with large and pleasant halls and rooms gay, healthful and pleasant to look upon. The floors are oiled. The doors are decorated! From the dressing-room one enters the bath-room where are two rows of troughs, with dripping boards round and douches. At bathing times the water is heated to 95 degrees Fahrenheit, cooling down gradually ends at 65 degrees Fahrenheit. The whole installation cost only £150. Dr. Kuntz, the school doctor, reports, " The general results have been very satisfactory." All the class teachers and medical officers affirm that the appearance of the children is fresher and healthier and that the air in the school-room is greatly improved. And he adds, " This is true especially in all older schools, where the ventilation is less efficient than in the modern ones. The children show a distinctly increased capacity, and zest for learning. In school bathing, much depends upon the interest and energy displayed by the class teachers."

(This last pronouncement is just as true in England as in Germany. Success in England may almost be measured by the interest of the head teacher, and where there is failure it is almost entirely because his or her co-operation has not been solicited or where it is not offered.)

Of the beautiful Schiller Schule, in Karlsruhehe, the Report says: "In this school of 1300 children, there is bathing always, summer and winter. Sixteen children bathe at a time; 200 daily, or up to 1000 a week. The bath-room has two long parallel troughs and rose douches; no cells or boxes, only forms and hooks for clothing round. . . . In school corridors there are 'crystal spring' drinking fountains: tasteful decorations, beautiful gymnasium with grand piano." The authorities testify: "The school air has been greatly improved since the introduction of baths: zest and capacity for work have increased. . . . In many cases the cleanliness taught at home by bathing has caused improved sanitary conditions at home. Every modern school without exception should be provided with shower-baths."

The third and last example here taken will be the beautiful Fluhrstrasse School at Munich. It is situated in a difficult area. All the bathing arrangements are under the control of the teachers. The children from six years old upwards bathe—80 per cent of all bathe regularly. "The dressing-room has forty-four boxes, 6 feet high, 3 feet deep, and the partitions, of varnished wood, are two or three inches clear from the floor. The bath-room floor has small red tiles, and the bottoms of the troughs are tiled. Coarse matting is laid down in the passages. . . . The girls wear a sleeveless gown of white and blue striped cotton." Here, as elsewhere, the testimony is that the bathing has resulted in a great improvement of the school atmosphere, in increase of zest for work and mental energy in the children, and a steady gain in self-respect, which must end in placing a great gulf between the past and the future of tens of thousands of citizens.

School bathing was begun thirty years ago in the schools of Mannheim. Since then it has spread all over Germany, and is now almost as much a part of the curriculum as are the three R's. It is not difficult to see some relation between it and the smallness of the percentage—not much more than 1 per cent— of neglected children in the Fatherland, only 1·8 per cent, while here, in England, in some districts the percentage is, not 1, but in some areas 50, 60, and 75 per cent of all the scholars. (Dr. Crowley, of Bradford, estimates that 35 per cent of school children are in an utterly neglected state—very verminous— and only 30 per cent very clean.) What a real saving these new bathing installations must represent, how they must tend to depopulate hospitals, and convalescent homes and asylums, and shelters for the decrepit and unfit, we shall try to show later, through comparative figures.   The German nation is beginning to focus its energy in the schools as a centre for the *prevention* of disease, and by-and-bye, though, despite the economical ways of the German nation, the cost of schools may grow, yet there will be a saving in other departments.   Early *prevention* will take more and more the place of cure, and early prevention is a pleasant thing—a matter of pure air, flashing water, sunny spaces, a kind of teaching and training that is almost perforce gentle. Such a training has lovely bye-products—is very rich in these.   One need not be an optimist to prophesy that it must sooner or later re-create the atmosphere, not of schools only, but of homes and cities.

.   .   .   .   .   .

It is said that skin diseases disappeared rapidly at the school bath centres.   But apart from the more familiar order of good result from washing there are others, less familiar, less direct.   We may be allowed to turn aside here for a moment to glance at some

of these. Misfortune has opened the door as usual
to this kind of study, and there have not been wanting persons in every age, who answered to the still,
beckoning finger. There have been, as we can see,
doctor teachers in all ages. A very notable group
of these were active in France at the end of the
eighteenth century. One of these, Father Itard
(he was a priest, though he did the work of a doctor)
had a strange pupil, the wild boy of Aveyron, and
was led through him to make a study of the lower
senses—touch, taste, and smell.

Many people know the story of the wild boy of
Aveyron! How one day three French hunters,
looking for game in a wood, came across a naked
boy of twelve, who fled from them like a wild beast
and tried to hide himself in a tree. In point of
fact he was a wild human being, and perhaps the
hunters had heard rumours of him. In any case
they ran after him, captured him, and carried him
off to a village, where they put him under the charge
of a poor widow. The poor woman did not know
very well how to deal with him, and he very soon
escaped from her and ran back to the woods. There
he roamed free for a while, but one very cold day
he wandered, as hungry wolves sometimes do, very
close to human habitations. He even ventured into

a house at last and was "captured" again and carried off to Paris. There he was kept as a kind of show, and was stared at and wondered at; but as he proved after a while to be not at all amusing, people got tired of him. The good priest, Father Itard, saw him at last and took him home, determined to educate him and restore to him his lost humanity.

Perhaps no one ever had a better chance of seeing what it means to have the doors of the lower senses half closed than had Father Itard. It goes without saying that the wild boy had had no human ear and eye training. It was not wonderful that he could not listen to music or human speech, that he observed nothing in his path that was not an obstacle or a fancied beast of prey, that he never walked, but ran or bounded along so that his teacher had to keep flying in the rear when he went out with him. But the most striking thing of all about him was the dullness of the *lower* senses. He had twenty-six deep wounds in his body, but he did not know how he had come by any of them. He could not feel when a thing was embossed or flat, when it was rough or smooth. As the skin is the organ of temperature this sense—of temperature—was lost with the rest. He would take up burning coals with his fingers, and take boiling potatoes out of the pot and stuff them into his mouth. The companion senses of touch, taste and smell, were so dull that the most delicious fragrance gave him no pleasure, and he swallowed disgusting things without any feeling of revolt. He could not fix his eyes, nor walk like a human being, nor shed tears, nor feel when he was bruised or burned. His restoration to humanity appears to have come through the education, first of all, of the lower senses, baths, massage, and treatment by an electric battery; and as this treatment began to take effect, taste-training through the offering of sweet and bitter things. Groping his way in the darkness (for little was then known of brain physiology in its relation to education), Itard succeeded after a time in awaking the dormant areas of this neglected brain, so that the wild boy began to feel heat and cold, consented to put on clothes (at first he ran naked in the garden in mid-winter), walked like a human being on two feet and with measured steps, shed tears, showed signs of gratitude, and joy, and sympathy, and even began to learn to speak.

Sometimes the lower sense doors are closed violently, and then there is sudden panic and breaking loose in what we may call the upper stories of the brain. "A young man, clever and rational," says one doctor, "suddenly gave himself to the worst tendencies. It was found that the sense of touch was lost, and he felt nothing at all." Later, sensibility came back to the skin, and in the same moment the moral nature righted itself—like a ship that, having been wedged in a frozen sea, finds again the water rising and falling below it, and spreads its sails to the breeze.

"What of this?" some may cry. "The children of the people are not wedged in polar ice." Fair and delicate are the babes born even in the darkest slum ; soft is the baby-skin as a rose-leaf, and sensitive as the young aspen. The question is, however, not whether the babe is born sensitive, but whether he is allowed to *develop* as a sensitive being. Dr. Leslie MacKenzie found that the sense of smell was not blunted in the children he tested. But it is possible, nay likely, that the dulling of smell takes place later. Matthew Arnold said that the upper class were a little like barbarians, the middle class wanting in idealism, and the people lacking *in feeling*. Where does this apparent want of feeling begin? It begins, of course, in the skin. "We all know," says Luys, a great brain specialist, "how fine, delicate, and sensitive is the skin of woman in general, and particularly of those who live in idleness and do no manual work . . . how their minds are continually informed of a thousand subtleties of which we men have no notion. In idle women of society and men with a fine skin mental aptitudes are developed and maintained in the direct ratio of the perfection and delicacy of sensibility of the skin. The perfection of touch becomes in a manner a second sight, which enables the mind to feel and see fine details which escape the generality of men and constitutes a quality of the first order, *moral tact*, that touch of the soul as it has been called, which is the mark of people with a delicate skin, and whose sensory nerves, like tense cords, are always ready to vibrate at the contact of the slightest impressions."

This is all very well for the lady (it is *so* well for her that the *tact* she gains will often take the place of all the talents); but what about the " horny-handed son of toil "? "Compare the thick skin of a man of toil," continues Luys, "used to handling coarse tools and lifting heavy burdens, and see if, after an examination of his intellectual and moral sensibility, you think that he understands you when you try to waken in him some sparks of those delicacies of sentiment that are so very striking in people with a fine skin. On this point experience has long ago pronounced judgment, and we all know that we must speak to everyone in the language he can comprehend and that to try to awaken in the mind of a man of coarse skin a notion of the delicacies of a refined sentiment is to speak to a deaf man of the sweetness of harmony, and to a blind man of the beauties of colour."

A great deal of rough work has to be done in the world, and this rough work is so far from being fatal to man's development, that it is pretty certain that no one has been really educated who at some time in his life has not done his full share of it. Yet to make the flesh rock is to shut life's doors, and to make it hard in childhood is to put up the shutters at daybreak.

Full sensory development implies, of course, the keeping fine of the lower senses—touch, taste, and smell—a literal "fine life below stairs" in the organism. It depends on clean air, pure water, abundant light, food that does not offend or degrade the palate, fragrance, but nothing to dull the sense for odours ; and last, but not least, *the habit of attending to sense impressions.* By such means the whole surface of the body becomes more responsive, less hide-bound, and thrills at the presence of subtler influences. It seizes undertones of life, and reaps new harvests of sensation. But who can buy all

these things? To-day in cities only the rich can buy
them. Almost any one can buy sermons or books;
any one almost can listen to lectures and concerts
and visit picture galleries. The things that are
wanted for the education of the *higher* senses are
cheap and popular. But the things that are needed
for the education of the lowlier senses are still very
expensive, in cities at least, and expensive things are
for the few. Many good things must be commun-
alized first in the schools.

.   .   .   .   .   .

The Americans, always practical, having realized
this, have begun the systematic training of the
lower senses so long ignored. They have begun it,
not only in schools, but also in reformatories. In
Elmira the whole treatment of the prisoner constitutes an appeal, not to the conscious, but to the
unconscious part of him; it is a descent into the
lower stories of life for the rekindling and restoration of the culprit's moral life there. Baths and
massage are given, and physical exercises that have
as their aim the inducing of a new sensitiveness.
The diet is supervised with the same end in view.
In England the prison is hygienic only in a very
elementary sense. The conditions favour the main-

tenance of normal health in dull organisms! But in Elmira the avowed aim is much bolder. And there is evidence that the treatment has the desired effect, for in many cases the dullard criminal, incapable of remorse at the time of entrance, begins later to show signs of pity and repentance. The stone melts. The heart becomes flesh. The life of the emotions is reached. The nearer goal—that of the *sensory* nature—is touched by methods that are partly mechanical.

.   .   .   .   .   .

In the school such methods are believed to be unnecessary. And of course it is true that no average child needs the radical kind of sense training dealt out to hardened criminals. But a child has something to lose—and a great deal to gain—from the lower sensory standpoint. America has no health centres in the ordinary school, and her appeals to the subconscious are not much more deliberate than are our own in so far as the basal sense of general touch is concerned. But the education of the sense of smell is carried on in many schools. Teachers armed with odorous things, flowers, spices, gums, sweet-smelling woods, test the range of smell in each pupil and develop the attention power given to this sense.

Besides this formal, there is much informal training —the frequent appeal to smell in the lessons on chemistry, botany, or domestic science.

As for taste, the difficulty of keeping this sense delicate and healthy is often great, on account of the indifference of parents. It appears that no sense is more easily depraved and coarsened than is this one, and the mischief once done can hardly be undone. One authority declares that the sense of taste cannot be redeemed even a little in less than nine months— that one must have nearly three hundred meals in order to forget a sensation produced by a harmful dish (such as tinned fish drenched in vinegar), or rather in order to enjoy a good article of diet. Thus a slum child, rickety and starving, will refuse to touch milk. Many will go hungry rather than swallow wholesome soup, and only after months will a depraved palate begin to tolerate the new food that, under natural conditions, it would have preferred from infancy. But this restoration of taste is certainly a greater triumph than the mastery of the art of spelling, and it will probably have more far-reaching results. It betokens a returning sensitiveness which will be its owner's best safeguard from degrading vices. And it is well to know that although fine taste is kept by few (Tolstoy draws attention in one of his books to the fact that men do not like sweets, and that to like sweets is nevertheless a guarantee that depraved tastes have not been acquired, or otherwise the innocence of the palate would have been lost), yet it is recovered by some— in childhood. *When dinner-tables are laid in the schools of the people, a whole range of new and far-reaching educational opportunities will begin to present themselves.*

Meantime, American primary education is interesting, not in what it has copied from other systems, but in what it is unconsciously putting forward in the way of new and untried experiment. The *direction* of these efforts is above all interesting. It seems to have some direct relation to the latest teaching of physio-psychology, yet without claiming such teaching as its stimulus or guide. Here, in the unconscious, lie its *radical* tendencies—its suggestion of new and bold flight in the future. For in thus dealing at last with the education of the lowly senses the Americans are beginning to develop in children a responsiveness that will make slum life and its horrors intolerable to all.

There may be still persons who will say that it is wrong to make *any* kind of life intolerable, and whose ideal of education is the fitting of children for any lot—however hard, bitter, and to healthy beings, unbearable. But the number of persons who hold such views must be growing smaller every day. For to most people it is getting clearer that the measure of responsiveness in any being is the measure of his *power.* "He that hath ears, let him hear." To those who can hear it is a friend who calls—to those who can receive, it is a friend who enters. "*The whole universe,*" said Thoreau, "*is on the side of the sensitive.*"

And we are all born sensitive—peasant's child as well as princeling, beggar and king, and out of this sensitiveness, which appears at first as mere weakness, all the higher kinds of energy are evolved. Sympathy, intellect, self-control, intuition, genius— all take their rise in it, draw their underground supplies from it. Thus it would seem that Carlyle is literally right when he says that the materials for human virtue, far from being rare, are "everywhere abundant as the light of the sun," since everywhere, in the rudest places, children are born, *not* hidebound, but with a delicate, receptive organ for covering. For a little while they can lose and yet recover their sensitiveness. Nature seems loath to let them finally be hardened—despoiled of their humanity. They gather, they even re-gather, "materials of virtue." For a little while. Then it is too late. "O woe and loss and scandal that they are so seldom elaborated and built into a result—that they lie unelaborated and stagnant in the souls of millions."

D

CHAPTER II

DEFECTS AND THEIR CONSEQUENCES

NOTHING is more strange and touching than is the part played by the defective child in the history of education. Long ago the feeble minded as well as the insane were treated sternly. It seems that people felt they were to blame in some way for their misfortunes. Even among those who did not blame them, there were many who thought that the feeble minded are a burden. A burden of course they are. But through an impluse that some call unreasonable the most forlorn found helpers, and then it was found that even the very defective can be of great use, and not only in small, but in great ways. Many processes, so rapid that they cannot be observed in the well endowed, are slowed down as it were in the feeble minded. And so these in a sense became benefactors of the race.

The first real teachers of the feeble minded were physiologists. Not of course that they were all medical men. Some were priests like Itard, and some were artisans. But the great teachers stand out from all others in that they began their work by studying the physical side of education. A great many of course, such for example as Esquirol and Pinel, who began in Paris the study and treatment of so-called idiots and insane persons, were doctors by profession. In England and Scotland too, doctors took up this new work, and certainly no one disputed their right to do so. For the professional teachers did not want to spend time and talent on children who, as it seemed, could never do them any kind of credit. Even the Scottish dominie, successful as he was, cared mainly for the "boy o' pairts," not for the poor "innocent" who ran about the village. So it came to pass that the school doctor has really come to us viâ the sad class rooms where the unfortunates of the race were gathered at last.

One of the most original and successful of these teachers was Edouard Séguin—a Frenchman living in America. He was a fully qualified doctor. He seems to have known very well all that was written up to his day—he died about twenty-five years ago, in the early eighties—by the great educationists. He was an admirer too, of Froebel. But it was from his poor scholars themselves that Séguin learned what made it possible for him to become a true pioneer.

He received into his school children before whom
Pestalozzi, Rousseau, Herbart, and Froebel would
have turned away in despair, and the study of their
works certainly could not help Séguin to discover
what he should do for them. So, even though he
was well acquainted with all the educational books
of his time he seems to have taken his medical
knowledge as the real basis of his work.

In his book, *The Child, Normal and Abnormal,*
there is a photograph of a child whom Séguin
received into his school. This child was about

nine years old when the photograph was taken.
A helpless, almost motionless being. His arm is
stiff—the hand and fingers wooden looking; the
mouth hangs open (it is left as it was when he
last stopped speaking). The eyes are fixed. It
would be useless to coax this child's attention by
appeals to the higher senses, and Séguin did not
attempt anything of the kind. He began the boy's
education by doing for him what the ordinary child
does without any help. He took the stiff arm and
began to move it up and down from the shoulder—
then exercised forearm and wrist, and finally invented
or rather copied (from the normal child) forty hand
exercises. And by dint of all this hard work,
carried on at first from without, and quite mechanic-
ally, the sleeping brain of the child was awakened,
the frozen limbs began to live, to move. Those
brain areas where movement is registered having been
awakened by such movements, the thrill of life
passed to higher levels, and a ray of intelligence
began to shine in the vacant eyes.

Here is a portrait of the same child after nine
months' education—if education it can be called—
that treatment which he received in the first days
almost as passively as an almost drowned man
receives the attentions of those who are trying to

bring him back to life. The face is so changed for the better as to be almost unrecognizable.

Séguin had a great horror of routine, and of falling into mere use and wont. His book, *The Child, Normal and Abnormal*, is like a living raft, and the reason is, that even though he sat at the feet of many teachers, he returned always to study the child under his own roof, to learn from the little helpless, and perhaps motionless figure of the "abnormal" child, whose pitiful face and form held the key to so many enigmas, whose darkened life was a secret as well as a tragedy. The study of the normal and the abnormal side by side proved very fruitful. When one begins to look into the exercises he gave to his defective scholars one finds, as we have already said, that he was just following the order in which a normal child develops. For example : the healthy infant, as soon as he can make other than reflex movements, begins to move his limbs by lifting the arm from the shoulder. The brain first takes control of the limb *as a whole*, then it takes control of parts ;

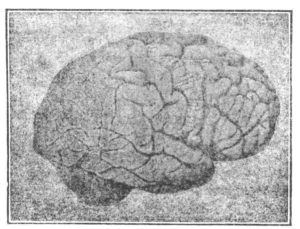

it takes finer and fuller control—all in a definite order. This order can be followed by a glance at any map of the brain where the areas of the motor brain, governing movements of various parts of the body, are shown.

Séguin followed this order, and he gave his reasons. But though brain physiology was not so far advanced in his day as it is in ours, for many years after his death, and even to-day, the natural order of growing control is violated in some infant schools all over the world. Yes, one may even yet find places where little children are forced to try to get control of their fingers in writing small letters long before they have real control of the larger arm and elbow muscles. Reform is slow, not because people have never heard of new methods, but because they do not know the meaning of them. For example: when the exercise, known as "arm-drawing," began to be advocated, there was an extraordinary amount of misunderstanding about the real meaning of it. It was believed to be a new and spurious kind of art! It was believed to be a trick—a fad—and also an entirely "new" order of exercise, never attempted before! Only after years did people begin to see that it was no more a new kind of art than is skipping, no more a new order of exercise than is walking or crawling, that its uses are physiological and that one may, and as a rule must, quickly pass beyond the need for it as the power of control becomes finer and more delicate.

Yet Séguin had gone far to demonstrate all this in his school thirty years ago, and to expound it in his books, *L'Idiotie* and *L'Enfant Normal and Abnormal.*

The phrase "a defective person" was once commonly believed to mean an idiot, or a person with no brain-power at all. But it is now known that every human brain is defective more or less, just as every world or planet is "defective." A world may have many fertile places and be very beautiful on the whole, but it is certainly not equally fair and equally fertile in every part. No more is any human brain. It is said that Mozart could not cut his own food, that a certain learned professor never could be trusted to take his own train ticket, and that Darwin lost any faculty for music he had ever possessed.[1] Some children are defective in ways that make it impossible to take the ordinary school curriculum, and yet they are not necessarily of low mentality, but are sometimes above the average.

For example. In 1906 a little boy of ten was taken into a "Special Class" in Bradford. He was intelligent; his blue eyes had a strange, sad look— a look of resignation and wonder. He seemed to be looking always for a deliverer, but to have lost all hope of finding him, and indeed, twenty years ago,

[1] "There are," writes Dr. Thomas, "many persons who are physically without the power of registering musical memories, although the ears are perfect. If such people lived in a world where musical memories were the only means of intercourse—in a grand opera world —they would be considered imbeciles."

he might have continued to look in vain. He was dumb. He had never spoken ; his hearing was good, and all the vocal organs perfect. At the age of five, he was sent to a school for the deaf ; but after some years the teacher sent him away, declaring that his hearing was very good, but that, seeing he would never utter one word, he was probably an idiot.

The boy then found himself in a class for the feeble-minded. He soon became a source of great joy and profit to his poor comrades, for he had just the kind of gifts that could make it possible for him to stimulate and interest them. So though he could not be a pupil teacher, he was something very much better. Armed with a piece of chalk, he would stand before the blackboard, and draw donkeys with panniers, horsemen riding upon horses, dogs begging for crusts, and cats, with handsome tails, chasing mice in a barn. The children stood round and looked at him with an attention which even skilled teachers could not perhaps have roused in them, and sometimes the head teacher came to watch the drawing, and even Her Majesty's inspector was known to join the group.

Not Froebel or Herbart, if they had risen from the dead, could have delivered him. The deliverer was at hand in the person of the school doctor.

In 1861 Broca, the Columbus of the brain, discovered that a certain part of the brain was diseased
in persons suffering from speech defects—that is to
say he discovered a speech centre. But since that
time it has become clear that speech involves activity
not in *one* part of the brain, but in many. Thus there
is a place where the sound of the spoken word is
received, another place where it is stored; then there
is an attention centre far away, but in connexion
with the storage place, and all these various parts
must be active and healthy before a word is heard,
stored, and attended to. Now the mechanism being
so involved, there may be a breakdown at one point
or another. One may be deaf through the ear, or
through the memory chamber, or through the higher
brain. The "word-deaf" boy, now in question, was
not deaf in the ordinary sense; and he was intelligent, so the attention centre was not in fault. *It
was the storage place that was lacking in his brain.*
It could not be restored, so another kind of memory
must take the place of it. Speech-training was
given him through the muscular sense. The child
took to the new method joyfully, and learned in a
day or two to say such explosive words as "pen"
and "penny." He got on fast. His father, who is
a cabinet-maker, says he will make a capital

workman. When a question is asked him he repeats
it noiselessly with his lips before he can understand
it; but he has made good progress, and speaks and
sings too, though with expressionless tones very like
a phonograph.

Then there are not only various kinds of word-
deafness; there are at least two kinds of word-blind-
ness. In one of these the storage place for written
words is damaged. In the other this storage place
is intact, but there is no access between it and the
visual path. Such a case often becomes an enigma
to all. The word-blind child may be clever, good
at hand work, quick and responsive, and perhaps to
complete his extraordinariness he is gifted with a
splendid visual memory, draws well, has a good
memory for numerals, and is good at arithmetic.
Dr. Thomas describes one of these children. The
teacher, bewildered by the boy's intelligence, yet
declared he must have a poor memory, since he
could not remember how to make letters! Alas!
it was not will power that was wanting. He strove
hard to learn to read, but all in vain. His writing
to dictation was a puzzle—every word wrong, mere
meaningless groups of letters. His teacher did her
best for him. He was so quick at arithmetic, and
could multiply figures so rapidly on the blackboard,

that she was completely puzzled. Has the brain then different storage places for letters and numerals? It appears so. And there are varieties of even this strange defect, for there are children who can learn their letters, but stick (for a good physiological reason) at the combinations of them!

What would have been the treatment of such children long ago? What is the treatment they receive in some places even to-day? No doubt they would have been, no doubt they still are, punished. For punishment is a short cut towards many supposed goals, and the tradition of it has come down, sanctioned by the authority of wise men, who knew no more about the brain than Plato knew about Lake Michigan! "There are all degrees of word blindness," writes Dr. Kerr, "from the ordinary bad speller to the individual who cannot recognize any word." And there are all degrees of word-deaf people, from the person (so common!) who has difficulty in remembering what he has heard to the person who cannot remember spoken words at all in the ordinary way. And the failure of these is not the result of the activity of the old Adam in them, but of weakness and defect. It may be overcome in part—or it may be altogether beyond the power of the victim or his friends to improve matters. In any case it is well, not only for the word deaf and word-blind, but for all children, that the school doctor has begun his investigations, and is making a tour, as it were, of the brain. The geography of the earth is pretty well known, the geography of the brain is in its infancy; still, the explorers have come at last. They are at the door of the school. They try to understand the growing brain, the energizing brain of school children. And as one by one its secrets begin to be yielded up, a new spirit of tolerance begins to enter the modern class room. It is born from observations made possible, sometimes by disease, but nearly always by some kind of sorrow, defect, or failure. It is sometimes an infectious disease caught in childhood—that strikes one note or another of the nervous system mute, or breaks (as in the case of Helen Keller) many strings. But in any case it is nearly always failure and disaster of some kind that lays bare new secrets of nerve mechanism. So tragedy is brightened by the fact that the greatest sufferers help many. Their trembling hands bear a gift. It is they who, more than others, explain the faults and failures of the well endowed.

One of the most crying needs to-day is the need for a school for the study of the abnormal. A school where defects, that may, or may not, constitute mental inferiority can be studied, and where physiological methods of teaching may be put to the test. At the mere mention of such a school some may object, on the ground that it would be a kind of inhumanity to experiment in training. But alas! What have we been doing always, what are we doing now, but experimenting?—and always more or less in the dark. In the new order of school, the experimenting would be done under safer conditions, and with a more definite end in view—that is all. The students would be more or less experts. Abnormal children would be under observation (for the school would be residential). They would not simply have easy lessons—which is only an evasion. Each would have the physical training (exhausting for the teacher as it often is) of which he was in need. Many problems that puzzle the ordinary teacher would, we may hope, be cleared up as the result of the work, for the new knowledge gained would be put within the reach of all schools, and even of every parent.

To-day, even in the best institutions, the doctors of the feeble minded and defective prescribe treatment, and supervise education. But there is no provision made for research work, or the application of the most recent discoveries in the methods of teaching, and this deprives the work of its highest value as well as of its greatest interest.

.   .   .   .   .   .

We have seen that some people, who are notably defective, are yet very far from being inferior to the average in mental or moral qualities.   They are like people, who being rich, have not access to some shops.   But of course *all* " defective " persons do not belong to this class.   There is a class of children who are *not* defective, but are very dull.   And there are some who are dull and also defective.   In short, every degree of dullness, and every variety of defect, may be found in schools.

To-day the classifying of children is carried out in a rough and ready fashion, but the advent of the school doctor has already had its effect.

Dr. Kerr has drawn a diagram to indicate roughly the variations of mental power in school children to-day.

In the middle are the normal children, probably from 60 to 70 per cent of the whole.   To the right are the very bright children, 10 per cent, and a small fraction for the genius.   To the left are the dull and backward, and beyond these a much smaller class—

the imbecile and idiot class. So difficult is it to draw hard and fast lines, however, that it is impossible to claim on this or any other table that it is really accurate. Moreover, there are many children whom one can hardly place anywhere. For some of these new names have been invented, such as "higher-

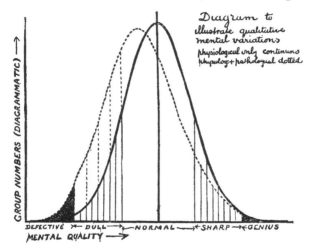

grade imbecile," "middle-grade imbecile," etc., and for others no name has been invented and no classification attempted.

The schools of 1870 were built for the normal child, and that was quite right, since the normal are the majority. A great mistake was made, however, when it was assumed that all children could be

E

normal if they liked, and that all teachers could force them into the ranks of the majority.

To begin with, let us take the children who certainly might become normal, and are not—those who cannot keep up with the others for causes that *might* be got rid of. They form a large group. From 15 to 20 per cent of all perhaps, are dull *simply through illness* or bad conditions of life. A great many of these have a stupid look, and pay no attention to any lesson. A great many suffer from adenoids, and some are dull and backward because they are ill, or in a chronic state of discomfort, strain, or depression because of bad feeding, bad air, want of sleep, and the burden of a life passed under difficult conditions.

In some German cities, such as Mannheim, this section of all the child population is provided for. Intermediate schools are opened for them—schools which are really health centres. There baths are provided, and excellent ventilation. The class rooms are sunny, the classes small. The education of the senses and the motor cortex is carried on vigorously, and deliberate efforts are made to awaken the higher centres of the brain. And this experiment is very successful. Spurious defects soon yield to it. The causes being removed, the effect ceases. In a few months many of the children are no longer dull. They begin to troop back to the ordinary schools. A certain number of them turn out to be even clever children. It is strange to think of! From 10 to 20 per cent of all school children would profit by this kind of schooling, a schooling which rewards the teacher so well that the child soon passes beyond it. But there are not yet many towns where this large class of children have been provided for. In most schools they still drag on with the rest—the last in everything, always behind! And few ever know that they too have wings, though they cannot fly. A much more hopeless class (a class which can progress, but very slowly, and of which few can ever go back to the ordinary school) receives attention, while *they* are often allowed to drift from " spurious " dullness into real and hopeless stupidity.

To come now to the really sub-normal, the genuinely dull and feeble minded. They are happily a much smaller class—not 3 per cent of the whole,[1] yet small as this class is, the type of inferior brain varies in different parts of the country. For example, there is one called the Mongol type. These

---

[1] The lowest grade of child, known as the idiotic is, of course, a still smaller group—a decimal fraction per cent of the child community.

children have fine textured hair and skin, almost almond-shaped eyes, small round heads, and a thick tongue. They are fairly common in London, but are rarely found in the North of England. On the other hand, there is the *Cretin* type of child, who has "a dry, harsh, yellowish skin, with hard, wiry, coarse hair, very placid, with thick spade-like hands." This type of child is believed by Dr. Kerr to be very much more commonly found in the North than in London. Perhaps the reason may be that exhaustion produces one type of dullard (thus the Mongol children are usually born late in the life of the mother) while lack of natural stimuli may affect the offspring in quite another way. In any case it is pretty certain that within small areas even children vary almost as greatly as do sometimes the seams of a rock. In a single county—the West Riding of Yorkshire—the type of feeble-minded child presents strange contrasts.

Still there are signs which are more or less common to the children belonging to the sad army of the feeble minded. "A highly arched palate, unsymmetrical head, a want of volume about the frontal region, irregularities about the ears (which are sometimes blue, ill-shapen, very large, and standing out from the head) incurved little fingers, webbed fingers,

with more than the usual number of fingers," all these
are mentioned by Dr. Kerr in his pamphlet on defectives as stigmata which are found very much more
often in the feeble minded than in other children. A
deeply seamed and ever-frowning forehead, an open
mouth, tight nostrils, are also common in them.
Every one of these signs tells something about the
unseen brain. And yet a great deal is left untold.
Some of these children are always surprising their
teachers and friends. One has an extraordinary
memory for certain things—remembers when trains
start or are due, finds things that are lost or remembers
things that were done and forgotten long ago by
other people. Some take a great interest in certain
things, such as horses, or ships, or fire-engines, or in
their father's trade. Some can draw better than the
child in the ordinary schools. They show you
vigorous sketches, of cows, dogs, and parrots, and
some (even among the more hopeless cases) can remember a great many airs, and can sing well and
even play on instruments. None, so far as I know,
have shown the usual amount of *inventive* power, or
have made tools and used them masterfully. Speech
offers a great many difficulties for a large number of
them. Through their various failings in language
we have indeed learned what a wonderful conquest

human speech is. More than a hundred years ago doctors were classifying mentally defective children by speech defects. Up to a certain point then, language, or connected speech, and beyond it tool projection, are final tests. They spell victory—the victorious arrival of the voyaging mind at the door of a new life, and that is why the study of the feeble minded leads up at last to the study of the tool projectors!

We have not to anticipate the tool projectors here however, in this chapter on "defects." We have to linger yet a little with the feeble, the unhappy minority. The family history of the seriously defective is very obscure. The parents do not want to lift the dark curtain that hangs over the past, and, in many cases they cannot. But enough is known to make it clear that alcohol—a poison that seems to have a strangely evil effect on the higher brain— is one great cause, if not THE great *direct*[1] cause of arrested development. Its work once fairly done, there is no going back on the consequences of it. They follow as the night the day.

The burden of supporting the unfit is heavy. Moreover, a certain percentage of all defectives are a constant danger to the people among whom they live.

[1] Very few would deny that the great indirect cause is poverty.

The moral imbecile is often clever enough, and out-strips every one at school. Then one day he may put all he learns to a terrible use. There is reason to think that certain chambers are missing in his otherwise well-built brain. As the teacher cannot create these chambers, it seems vain to bring fine furniture in the shape of good precepts. Perhaps one day doctors and teachers will know what to do. But to-day, the doctor can merely point out why society should protect itself. It is proposed that finger-print registers should be kept of all children who have had to come before a children's court—that is, before a body formed to deal with the crimes or serious offences of the abnormal. The fact that they are known would act it is hoped much as a conscience acts in the normal person.

It is pleasant to turn from these markings and finger prints that *betray*, to the tools and hand-work that reveals! Pleasanter to know that it is the revelation, not the betrayal, that is common. The betrayal is comparatively very rare. It is a promise and a prophecy, not a betrayal, that is in the work of the average man.

Of course it is not always fairly offered. It may be hindered or withheld for good reasons. Still, it should be there, and one day every educator will look for it; for self-projection in work—even in work of the roughest kind—represents the something that makes man not merely higher than the beasts, but different from the beasts. Long ago he began to use his hand, as no wing, no talon, no paw of an animal, however powerful, was ever used. He found expression through it, and not in one way alone. For though language[1] and manual work seem to have sprung far apart as representing two very distinct ideals in education, yet there is certainly no ground for this separation from the physical standpoint. Language is not only a projection, but it is a very early and simple one, and was almost certainly at first entirely one with that of the hand. Before words there were sounds, and before sounds gestures. And these gestures were already a preparation for activities whose real meaning was far above their mere immediate end. In short, the impulse that

---

[1] In an interesting paper on speech defects, Dr. Thomas points out *that all the four memory centres dealing with speech and for the performance* of delicate actions are stored in the brain in close proximity to one another. This is true also of the visual sense. But, what is even more significant, these centres are supplied with nourishment through the same artery. "It seems likely," writes Dr. Thomas, "that this community of arterial supply is of enormous importance. The great advantage arising from such automatic increase of blood supply is obvious. The right- or left-handedness of articulate beings may be dependent upon this fact."

made the human project his hand in tools, and
create even language at first through the hand, was
no mere development of brute force or brute cun-
ning. It was the impulse of a higher order of
energy, preparing for one knows not what future of
enfranchised and transformed power. And yet this
finer force, overflowing, as it were, in creative work,
was conditioned, so far as we may judge, by the
health, the fitness, of the striving worker. It was the
flower of a lowlier life. It may exist in the sickly ;
but disease tends to destroy it. It is found in the
defective, but not always. It is always manifested
by the healthy and normal individual.

Thus it is, for the educators of the normal at least,
the central factor and pivot of all training.

Yet it does not show itself at birth or in infancy.
It is evolved gradually, and declares itself only when
early childhood is fairly past.

The child under seven uses his hand in a hundred
different ways, but he does not, as a rule, project it.

But what, then, we may ask at this point, does his
activity mean—his almost feverish restlessness, the
restlessness that makes even the Jesuit teachers (so
anxious nevertheless to influence the young) glad to
leave him to his mother; a "self-activity" that

Froebel sought to use—what does this condition mean as a preliminary to the first rude efforts to project the hand? We may not linger over such a question, but we must attempt a brief, imperfect answer.

CHAPTER III

ART AS A PREPARATION FOR WORK AND TOOL-MAKING

THE YOUNG ARTIST AND HIS MODEL

THE key to the problems of human progress appears to lie in the realm of the *unconscious*. It is the new understanding of that dark realm that leads people no longer to look upon natural impulses as evil or meaningless. The young child cannot project his hand, but he uses it, and invents, or discovers rather, a hundred ways of using it, so that some teachers, as we have seen, have set themselves to copy them. He does not project his sense organs in instruments, but he loves, not only music, but noise, experiments even in painful ways (as when he draws a screeching pencil down his slate). He cannot project his muscles in fine mechanisms, but everyone knows how he experiments with muscles and even with joints.

He does not stop short entirely, however, at this point of mere activity and sensation. He gets a kind of acquaintance with his own anatomy by movement. But every one knows that at a certain age children want to draw, and also that for some years they show a very distinct preference for the living model, and will draw animals and men, even though these are the most difficult subjects of all and are hardly attempted by some grown-up artists, except in the way of caricature. Children of all nations and classes—Japanese children of the highest class as well as British children of the poorest class, cover walls, pavements, and books, with drawings of the human form, and also model this figure, too, with any material that comes handy—it may be mud, or it may be snow.[1]

The most " discouraged " and "disciplined" class of children in the world will cheer up suddenly if it is proposed to them to draw, not a cube, but say a cat—and will grasp pencil or pen with returning courage. If the teacher, or friend, however, can himself draw an animal, or still better, a man, their delight and admiration know no bounds. Unhappily, even the best teachers, with very few exceptions (but

[1] It is through man, too, that they approach the study, not only of art, but of the natural sciences and of Geography. "Children," as Kropotkin says, "care little for Nature if it has nothing to do with man."

these exceptions include Leonardo da Vinci) usually ignore this impulse, and offer few suggestions and little help to the mannikin-drawing children. The reason is not far to seek. Even very learned people are usually aware that they cannot draw a man very well, and they do not want to be asked to try. But writers on education, feeling perhaps secure that no one will require or expect *them* to draw the human figure, are not nearly so reserved about the child's selection of subjects.

Thus psychologists such as Sully have filled books with grotesque child drawings, and have traced their evolution, so that now many people know when to expect the appearance of ears and nose, of heels and elbows in the mannikins—also when to expect profiles showing two eyes and riders whose legs do not appear behind the horse's transparent body. It is noticeable, however, that in the case of most children, those embryo-like drawings, with their saw-teeth, rake fingers, and claw-like hands, do not give place to others of better proportions. They do not go on (though it is only a step) from the straight arm to the tapered one, or from the clawed hand to the human hand. On the contrary, they stop drawing quite suddenly, and nothing remains of the early and healthy impulse but a life-long conviction on the part of the little artist that he cannot draw.[1]

And yet, though the normal child's selection of a model is certainly very bold, it is strangely wise. For, when we begin to consider the human form we find that it is not only the measure of all things, but also that it is, as we said, a kind of store-house of originals. Within it, not without it, the great events take place. There, first of all, is elaborated everything which is to be flung forth at last and revealed in labour. All this is not a mere figure of speech. It is a simple fact, and it has been set forth already or alluded to by such writers as Zeizing, Virchow, and Ernest Kapp. And it is this amazing fact that makes the child's choice so significant.

But this is not all. The adult human figure and head, offers, in spite of many fallings off in individuals and even deformities, the best, the most

[1] The school doctor looks at a child's drawings, as he looks at a child's face or hand—that is, mainly to learn what he can about him. His interest in the drawing itself is a secondary thing. But the drawing reveals something about the artist—his touch, sight, memories, attentive power, etc.—so it is like the tool, a kind of book for him to read. As early art is very naïve, it is easier to read the meaning of child drawings, modellings, and inscriptions than might be supposed. It is proposed that at the International Exhibition of School Hygiene next year, a place shall be given to drawings, etc., as records, and to certain peculiarities in drawing, writing, and printing as symptoms.

varied illustration of the great law of the relations of parts—the key of the mystery of beauty and fitness. This law can be studied in crystals, in plants, animals, architecture ; but in none of these so perfectly as in the highest part (or head) of the human being, and in him only at the age when he has arrived at his full growth.

This law is, briefly, that in any form whatsoever a pillar, a building, a plant, a face, a gown, a pitcher, a vase, a pot, an axe, any two parts must stand to one another in the same relations that the larger of these stands to the whole.

The beholder does not *know* all this perhaps, any more than the infant musician knows that he selects the octave or the fifth. It is only because the law was illustrated a thousand times by thousands of unconscious workers and artists that it was at last appreciated and received its formula. It can be traced in the proportions of a horse's head, limbs, hind-quarters. But the higher forms of life give, of course, a fuller illustration of it than do any of the lower.

And the impulse of the child is, to begin with the form that illustrates it most completely—the adult human.

Strange to say, this adult form is not at all like his own.

His own body does not illustrate the law of fitness and beauty, though during the whole growing period it is striving to fulfil it. Below is a drawing from Zeizing of the newly-born child. The head is enormous, the upper part of the body long in

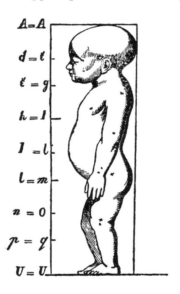

proportion to the lower. Every part seems to feel the force of gravity. To be sure the years that follow bring a great change in the proportions of the figure, so that at seven a child is as little like an infant of a week old as he is like a man of thirty years. The helpless, earthward-borne form is

lifted, as it were, in every part and made ready to be
a pedestal for the head, as well as an obedient, active

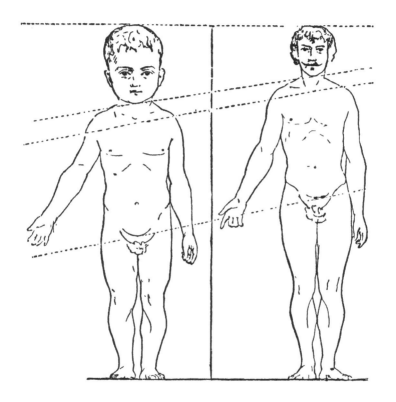

servant of the brain. Thus it will be readily seen
from the diagram above that the waist-line is much
higher in the seven-year old than it is in the infant,

F

and the neck-line too is lifted. But for long years the seven-year old will not fulfil the law in his members. And on many grounds the impulsion may be justified which makes a child pass by his own form, and also the form of hobbledehoys, to draw the adult face and figure.

Endless faces does every child scribble on his slate, without knowing anything about the law of beauty and fitness. These scribblings are usually wiped out and forgotten, but not always. There is now a movement on foot to encourage them, and to respect them. It is beginning to dawn on many that perhaps we have not seen, and do not yet see, the full meaning of this impulse to draw the human form.

CHAPTER IV

THE FIRST TOOLS, OR THE PROJECTION OF HANDS

MOVEMENT, play, art, are all a kind of preparation. They are all, but especially the last two, imitative in character, reflecting impressions received—and they are a preparation ; but for what ? For something that out-distances them all and is entirely different from every one of them. For tool-making.

A tool differs entirely from a picture, or statue, or any work of art, because it can be used as a member. It *is* used at first as a member, and, indeed, the earliest tool makers were not conscious of it as anything outside their own bodies.

The German, Ernest Kapp, was the first to show fully and in detail what the tool is. In his book, *Philosophie der Technik* (from which some of the following illustrations are taken), he shows how in remote ages man struggling for life with creatures stronger than himself and hardly lifted any higher

67

than they in the scale of consciousness yet began to do what none of them had done. No bird has made a new wing, no wild beast has forged a new tooth or paw. These do not project themselves. But this feeble creature, the ancestor of man, began to project himself, and in doing so climbed, as it were, out of that lower self, reached beyond it, and began to understand it.

It was certainly not the desire to know himself which induced the ancestor of man to make his first tool.[1] He wanted to strike, to pull, to tear—not to know himself! He stumbled on the new track driven by the primal hungers. His hand was doubtless very unlike the hand of the latter-day man— the fingers more locked or webbed, as they are even to-day in the hands of some children. And for ages the tools he made seem to reflect this hard narrow hand and locked fingers in the heavy stone axe, the stone hatchets and hammers of the stone period.

---

[1] The "rounding to a separate mind" is a slow process, and is going on to-day slowly, as in bygone ages. But the savage has still a much vaguer idea of his own frame as a separate thing than have civilized people. Mr. Dudley Kidd, in a book called *Savage Childhood*, tells how little Kaffirs beat the toys of those who have injured them. A grown-up Kaffir who had a headache believed that the pain was in the roof of the hut! And they can hardly locate pain, and are slow to learn what it means to hurt others. Thus the first tool-makers were probably as conscious of their tools as of their hands, and used one simply as a part of the other.

The point, however, is, that he began to project this hand that was not yet a hand.

A very prominent part of it would be the grasping, claw-like finger and finger-nail. These were destined to be projected in a great many positions, and in

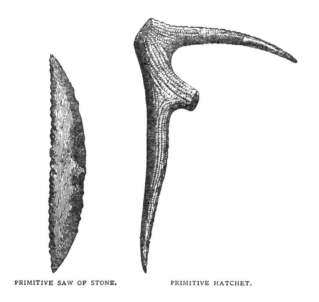

PRIMITIVE SAW OF STONE.   PRIMITIVE HATCHET.

finest detail. A knife is a broad, sharp nail projected; the saw is a set of nails, or perhaps teeth; and the primitive hatchet was a finger-nail and looks very like a talon, as did its maker's finger. The fist is a hammer. It must have been a narrow, sharp kind of hammer at first, for the power to close the hand depends on the power to open it, and there

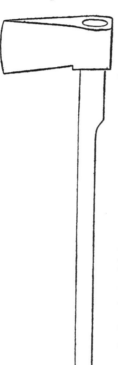

is good reason to think that the hand opened slowly. Opened it was, however; and the palm projected at last in the plane, and the hollowed palm in the cup and basket. Even the arm was projected at last as a lance, and also as a rudder and oar, which is the simple form of a stretched arm and flat hand. The moving arm is seen to-day in many work-shops, on the river sides, and lifting places; and the perfected human arm in beautiful tools. Still the impulse to perfect seems to be, for the most part, unconscious. Here is an early German axe.

In contrast to this heavy tool, that looks like a weapon, there is this drawing, from Kapp's book, of the axe of a modern American backwoodsman. The iron blade lies parallel with the shoulder and its powerful muscles, the elbow is parallel with the

outward upper curve of the handle. The wrist
corresponds to the middle of the inner curve, and

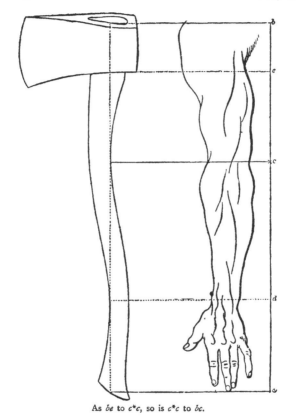

As *be* to *c*c*, so is *c*c* to *bc*.

the whole axe is, as Kapp has shown, a faithful copy
of its original model, and its proportions fulfil the

law of beauty, which is also the condition of greatest serviceableness. No child arm could project such an axe. But could there be a more useful exercise devised for children than the study (playful or otherwise) of this arm? To get, unconsciously, a right notion of its proportions is surely a good preparation for the unconscious projection of a tool that will fit it—and this is the kind of exercise that children will choose if left to themselves, and will persist in for a long time.

The meaning of this unconscious selection was not dwelt upon, or even noted perhaps, by Pestalozzi or Froebel, but it is not therefore a thing to be ignored by all who come after them.

CHAPTER V

THE CHILD-HAND TO-DAY

THE idea that manual work has a good effect on the whole body is certainly not new. Teachers saw the improvement long ago as a thing that could hardly be overlooked; and so when systems of work were drawn up for schools the delicate and defective children were not forgotten. There are special classes in woodwork arranged for these in various cities.

For years, then, before there was any talk of school doctors, teachers observed the good effect of some kinds of work; but they also noted the evil—the stunting effect of other kinds of labour.

For example, in Lancashire and Yorkshire there is still a large army of half-time and full-time children working in the mills. The conditions of factory life have been vastly improved in recent years, so from the point of view of sanitariness and humane treatment there is really nothing, as a rule, to complain of in the ordinary factory.　Yet the teachers report that from the very first day that he enters the mill the half-timer begins to lose all interest in school-work.　A subtle change comes over him which it is really very hard to define.　One would say that the organism is disappointed.　It was in full career, as it were, yesterday, making for a bright goal, and lo! suddenly it is stopped.　This is not a fanciful rendering of the facts; it is a statement borne out by the position which the children hold in the school before and after the date of beginning the mill labour, as well as their general behaviour and appearance.

And the teachers reported this for years.　They talked of it at their meetings; they wrote articles about it in their papers, and they carried on a very keen battle against child labour and half-time in the mills.

The teachers of evening schools, too, and those who interest themselves in young people, were not silent.　The noisy behaviour of the lads and girls in their off time, the horse-play of trippers, and the shouting and singing in excursion trains, had something in them that spoke more of defiant sadness than of gaiety.

Great sociologists joined the teachers who worked and wondered at the adolescent. They had seen the trippers ; but they had known some of them in child-hood, when they had been promising. Why were they so very disappointing in youth? And why did they lose ambition, hope, energy, power of attention, as they grew older? Charles Booth, in his *Life and Labour in London*, remarks that many bright boys of thirteen or fourteen who earn four or five shillings per week as milk carriers seem to grow out of all ambition as the years pass, so that at the age of sixteen or seventeen they are content to go on earning what is then a mere pittance—the wage of little boys. Later, as he points out, many of these become casual labourers or drift into the sad army of the unemployed.

What does it mean?—this disappointment of the organism. The question has to be fairly asked at last—and an answer looked for. The restlessness of the child should not end like the restlessness of the young animal—that is to say, in mere lethargy. The movement of life in civilized human beings of normal type and unchecked energy, should swing upward as time goes on into a higher order of activity, into an activity that cannot be followed, measured, and analyzed, not because it is slower, but because it is incalculably more rapid than the careering of animals or the flowing of rivers.

When this forward movement is checked, the result is something that is not to be argued with. The adolescent in whom it takes place cannot find any antidote for it in what is said to him, as a rule. He is as helpless to use words as a cure as he would be to use a peroration to turn back a threatened attack of influenza. His symptoms are faults, but they are mere symptoms all the same. Dr. Kerr has shown how the very violence of his mode of enjoying himself is the result of an instinctive need to flush neglected brain areas. But as for finding anew the zest and ardour of mental life, how is that to be done when the very material out of which it is born has been lost?

The advent of the school doctor has made it possible to study the real problems involved in these successes and failures in a new way, and with fresh courage. Every one of them has its roots in the growing organism—and the task before the school doctor is to discern these, and to set them in the light. Just as the home and hospital doctor has to know something of the mechanisms involved in eating and drinking, in swallowing and digestion, so the school doctor has to study the brain, the organ of mind, at all stages. He has to try to understand the mechanism involved in learning to read and to write, to draw and to dig, to read and to sing, to think and to reason; and above all he has to probe deep and even deeper into the secrets of progress and arrest.

Séguin, through his "defective" scholars, offered the first striking illustration that the brain is a transforming centre, that energy is not merely received there and travels there, but is changed as it travels. At different stations of this great "transformer" different degrees and forms of energy are worked up. At the outermost parts of the nervous systems some vibrations are quickly dispersed, and die away without waking any consciousness. Yet from first to last the nervous system is a conductor, a condenser, a transformer, and a detector. All the sensibility of the body is drained by it from the very outposts and is conducted along the nerve fibre as the electric fluid is conducted along the wires.

From fibre to fibre, as Luys has shown, from sensitive element to sensitive element our whole organism is sensitive, and the sum of feeling, rich or poor, that makes a sentient person, is conducted as a series of isolated currents into the general receiving centre of the Brain. There, what has been carried is fused, changed, transformed, and in that transformation everything is represented. There is a strange tenacity of the new life as regards all it has received or conquered. The brain at almost any period can store up impressions, as some kinds of metallic plates store solar rays, but in childhood the hold on these is all the surer because they are swung, as it were, into the general and rapid movement of a growing, energizing organ. If the material is stinted then, and if movement and experience are confined to one part of the organism, we have reason to think the mischief wrought will be final. We have reason to think this, not only from the teaching of brain specialists, but also from the experience of teachers as well.

During the past year Dr. Thomas, an assistant school doctor of the London Education Committee, has made an attempt to find out the real effect of overwork plus hand lethargy on the wage-earning children of London.

He began by making an examination of some thousands of children (unemployed children, that is non-wage-earning, and attending school regularly) so as to get figures which would serve as a standard of comparison when he began to examine wage-

earning children of the same age. To be sure
neither section of children, wage-earning, nor non-
wage-earning can be said to have much or varied
free hand labour, for even in schools the hand is
still apt to be rather severely snubbed. But in most
schools, and certainly in those that have manual
centres, the hand has more exercise than has that
of the message boy.[1] And the majority (though
not all) of London children who earn wages are
messengers of some kind, and earn their money by
going errands.

Dr. Thomas divides the wage-earning boys of
London into four classes viz. newsboys, milkboys,
boys employed by shopkeepers and small trades-
men, and barbers' boys. Four hundred boys were
selected by the teachers in fourteen boys' schools
widely scattered over London. Each boy was
examined and notes taken on the state of his health
—that is, of the existence, not of stupidity in the
first place, but of anæmia, severe nerve signs, deformities, and severe heart signs.

In so far as the general health of the average

---

[1] It has more varied exercises too than has the hand of the child
who enters a mill. For though a doffer or factory child does use his
hand all day long, it is but a very small group of muscles that is
brought into activity.

non-wage-earning child is compared with the wage-earner, the percentage is as follows:

Hours worked weekly.	Number of Boys.	Fatigue.	Anæmia.	Severe Nerve Signs.	Deformities.	Severe Heart Signs.
All schoolboys of districts (workers and non-workers)	3,700	—	25	24	8	8
Working 20 or less hours .	163	50	34	28	15	11
Working 20–30 hours .	86	81	47	44	21	15
Working over 30 hours .	95	83	45	50	22	20

These figures show the rapid deterioration of health that follow hard and monotonous labour in childhood. But as we are now concerned more especially with one effect of this labour—to wit, the *mental* effect of it—we will not linger over the general question. The interesting point in the Report to us at present is what follows.

"It may be suggested that these children are, to begin with, of an inferior type mentally and physically. But it was found that in two schools where the physique of the boys had been accurately noted, the children who went to do this kind of work were as follows :

	Numbers.	Considerably above average physique.	Below average.
Workers at School 1 . .	29	18	7
,, School 2 . .	40	23	11
	69	41	18

Thus though only 26 per cent were below the average physique, of these below the average more than half were exceptionally brilliant mentally, although 17 per cent of all were mentally below the average." " These results show," continues Dr. Thomas, " that this out of school work is a wanton dissipation of the children's powers, the chief national capital, and that the evil effect falls on the best of the children." It is seen to be a waste because the school work of the wage-earner deteriorates at once. It is so in London. It is so in Yorkshire. The bright eager boy who wanted to earn the rent and could learn fast becomes stupid and indifferent. Out of 330 wage-earning boys Dr. Thomas found that 86 were one standard, 83 two standards, 37 three standards, and 3 four standards behind that corresponding to their age.

Yet the conditions of life were not rendered worse, but as a rule *better*, for these children when they

G

started work. To begin with, they had probably
better food. Then in most cases they were out
more than before in the open air, and this tells
favourably in one way on the newsboys. But
even then it does not prevent the physique as a
whole from declining steadily. The boy is a walker,
a runner, a carrier. To walk, to run, to carry as free
exercise is good—but as work it spells mere blight
and loss. It was, by the aid, not of feet but of hands,
that human life was grasped ; the slowly opened
hand made the invisible path. It forged far ahead,
and pierced the narrow horizon of the brute. And
the organism, in a sense, knows when the upward
movement is checked, when the future that was won
is lost. No spring will revive the ambition of the
finished hooligan. It seems that Nature has fixed
the seasons of human growth as she has fixed the
seasons of animal growth, that it takes longer to
become a man than a beast, and longer to become a
civilized man than a savage (besides which the
savage has more time freely given him).[1] It is
possible in a garden to get to know what to expect
at different seasons. So it is possible in the school

[1] Thus the boys of New Guinea, for example, are not hindered from
making things. They rig up tents, build rude boats, make sails and
bows and arrows, and are as active in wood and wild as was Robinson
Crusoe.

garden to get some notion of the kind of thing
to expect at any period, to know, for example,
when the dexterity should appear that will one day
become intelligence, and when to look for that kind
of practical gift that will by-and-bye flower—it may
be in late days—into a power of abstraction.   It
must be possible to gain this kind of insight, or why
should the kindergarten have come at all?

And it must be possible to see at last why some
human plants will never flower at all—why the
movement of life does not swing upward, but decline
early, or refuse to mount; to see why a message
boy is content to be a casual or a loafer at last, and
to have no part in the stirring changes of the world-
garden.

All the while the human race is forging ahead
—or rather, the happier members of it are forging
ahead.   There is no mistaking the fact of projection
carrying them on, freeing them for new effort, and
the prophecy of unknown and undreamed-of secrets
of the organism itself shadowed forth in our projected
cable telephones and wireless telegraphy.   In this
whirlwind we call science, the favoured few are borne
forward, but in the stress of industrial life some of
the fittest are destroyed and flung aside.

CHAPTER VI

THE PROJECTION OF SENSE-ORGANS

THE EAR

THIS is an age of prodigies. One child after another appears in the concert room, and amazes the public by his or her powers as a violinist or pianist, and at public exhibitions of child drawings the man in the street hears with wonder that a little child is the artist who drew this or that picture. Yet the child prodigy is not a new thing. He has dazzled people for centuries. He is always an artist, a player, and, in rare cases, a composer. Sometimes he is a philosopher.[1] But he is never an instrument-maker —an artisan.

Long delay in the development of a musician is unnecessary, because the musical apparatus in his own body is perfected in all its parts soon after birth. For example, that part of the ear which is concerned with hearing more directly than any other,

---

[1] The child philosopher is, however, a forced growth, and his philosophy, though borrowed, is a weird product.

is full grown at birth, and long before a baby can
speak, its key board (or Corti's organ) is vibrating
with the activity of microscopic strings that analyse
and place myriad sounds and tones. What does the
baby know of all this? Nothing. He can sing—he
can play if there is nothing to hinder. If the right
stimulus is given, the music will begin. Tolstoy,
Hearn, and many others, have testified, after working
among children and peasants, that they are nearly
all capable of a wonderful musical development. If
this does not take place in many to-day, it is only
because there is something that actually hinders it,
or because there is nothing to call it forth.

We do not circulate our own blood, but it is
circulated in us. We do not consciously make our
food change into muscle and nerve, or bone; we are
not chemists, and we certainly could not, by taking
thought, elaborate all the juices and acids that are
formed in us daily. Yet those changes take place
in us. Just in the same way the peasants of Russia
or Scotland (to whom the greatest composers have
gone for their themes) do not "make" this music.
It sings in them. An instrument (which is, of course,
not a part, but the whole organism and its life) is
played on, and it pours forth its strange human
music like an æolian harp through which all the

winds of life are passing.   Sometimes a musical
parent, such as Mr. William Platt, listens and hears
his babies rediscovering the plagal cadence and
canon for themselves, and gathers material for
pianoforte pieces from their lips.   But much oftener
to-day the *real* music is stopped, and something else
is forced on the singer.   When the instrument is so
fine that it sings or plays in him almost from the
first, we have a " prodigy."

The point is that the original of all musical instruments is within us.   But when did *they*, like tools,
begin to be projected?   Long ago, for in the very
oldest books allusion is made to a variety of musical
instruments.   Perhaps the first was a horn (Mr.
Platt's children made one with paper), but it is
certain that the first instrument maker did not know
that he was shaping the eustachian tube in his own
throat.[1]

This tube, and also the tongue, the larynx, the
lungs, the ear-drum, all the outer and more obvious

[1] Mr. William Platt, who has written a short book on this, gives
examples of short, single-themed pianoforte pieces, a child's song, a
hymn, a double-themed duet, and a three-themed duet, the entire
material of which was gathered from the lips of young children. "One
terse piano solo of twenty bars is founded on a stirring theme by a
youngster of seventeen months, a child just striving to talk, and quite
incapable of doing anything with a pencil, except trying to swallow
it !"

parts of the human mechanism, were projected thousands of years ago, and yet without the aid of such instruments the people of many lands sang their sweetest songs. In the hands of young children, and indeed of older ones, an instrument is merely a hindrance. It may become a substitute, which is worse! Or it is used as a toy, or diverted from its purpose. And it is doubtless for one or other of these reasons that the greatest teachers, such as Tolstoy, do not care to see any instrument in schools.

Perhaps the first horn was a rounded hand. In any case the first horn or trumpet used by most children is their own rounded hands.

For a long time, though they enjoy instrumental music, and even mere noise, they have little impulse to make any other instrument than this. And so the *original* instruments are well used, and well nourished, they become stronger, and finer with use, and fall more under the control of the will.

From the very first, however, the impulse to project is a symptom of health, of vigour. It is not the child suffering from adenoids, or weakness of chest or throat, who wants to shout through his hands. It is the healthy child who experiences this need.

The instrument is projected then in the first place

only because the projection is needed. The musician needs a stronger lung, a larger lip, a bigger larynx. He wants, as does everyone in whom new power is generated, a greater body than his own, but one that is still his own. In this need and power lies the whole history of instrument making ; and in spite of disease (which balked so many), and weakness (which prevented myriads), this need seems to have become more imperious and profound, and the power to meet it greater ; for not only mouth and tongue, but larynx, windpipe, lungs, tympanum, all were projected in turn ; the forms of all these came forth in turn, and now appear, in spite of all disguises, in the orchestral instruments of to-day.

There was no halt in this revelation. Ranging far and farther into the recesses of the hearing organ, instrument makers began at last to make spinnets, then pianos, and piano organs. It did not appear at first that these could possibly have their prototype in the human body. But the physiologist arrived in due time, to show that this "original" existed within. He showed the organ, with three thousand strings, which forms a part of the inner ear. It is called "Corti's organ," after its discoverer. No one can look at it without being reminded of the keyboard of a piano. It is microscopic. No eye had seen it.

No one had imagined it. Yet it was flung forth like spray from the wave—in work.

Sometimes, perhaps, the secret is flung forth, but remains a secret. In the violin, for example, there is something that is never recognized, never explained. It is, above all, the old violins, the great old violins, which hold this secret, which is also a spell. Something in the heart of the violinist answers to it, and he loves it as he might love a beautiful mistress without understanding it. It is

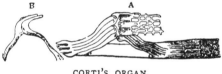

CORTI'S ORGAN.

said that the old violin makers did not want to tell their secrets, and so took them to the grave with them. But perhaps they did not even *know* them— but projected some wonderful part of themselves which afterwards, in others, never broke a way into the outer chambers of the workaday life.

The ways in which children's condition varies in different classes of the community are not always to be accounted for. It seems, at the first blush, as if the poorest and most neglected were not, after all, having the worst of it in every respect! But in so far as the higher sense-organs are concerned there is no possible room for doubt as regards the symptoms! The poorer and more neglected the group of children the greater percentage of injured eyes and ears does it furnish. We see this more particularly when we come to think of eyes.

Perhaps at first a child with deteriorating senses may strive to overcome his defects—may listen, and look eagerly, obeying an impulse that indicates how the door of the senses must be opened wide, and how this opening is a great part of the whole of the life of childhood. But very soon the effort, so often balked, becomes feebler. He resigns himself. The world narrows round him. *He* does not need to project that poor, unsatisfactory ear or eye. If in later life any instrument can help him it will be one which can be compared not to a tool, or projected hand and arm, but rather to a crutch that takes the place of a limb that has been lost.

.   .   .   .   .   .

The Eye![1] The part played by vision in mental life appears greater and greater as one looks below the

---

[1] The ascent of *eyes* is set forth very well by Dr. Mott. The mere film ; the independent rabbit-eye, fixed like a window in either side of a house ; the cat eyes, moving in harmony, with front limbs, and on to human vision—all the steps are described in a very interesting way.

surface and catches some real glimpse of the tissue of thought and also of the real nature of the great triumphs in art, science and literature. "Think of the beauty of the scenes," says Kropotkin, "of Tourguenieff's masterly novels. Every one of these could be the subject of a picture!" When Tourguenieff himself thinks of Shakespeare he thinks of him in a picture, and declares it worthy "of the brush of a painter." And what are Shakespeare's works to any of his lovers but a panorama—a series of wonderful pictures—beautiful as Tourguenieff's own novels? The scenes, the heroes, the heroines, the details of the novel or drama, are seen again by those who read them.

And this power of vision is something altogether distinct from the faculty that makes a bird or a rabbit keep clear of obstacles.

The great teachers know this so well that they almost instinctively pursue the pictorial method of teaching. That they can make the pictures visible is part of their greatness. But they do not despise aids. For example. In teaching geography to children the greatest geographers do not arm themselves with the best charts, models, and maps, before entering the class rooms. These things are useful to *them*, as students, but they are of use only in so far as the student can see clear pictures, through them, pictures painted in unfading colours ; and the child sees in them nothing but paper and clay. So Professor Geddes tries to make it possible for children to see the world by means of the panorama. He strove to get this realistic kind of picture for the children of Dunfermline. Other geographers engage the finest painters of the age to paint pictures of different scenes. The Libyan desert and its burning sands—the Rockies, a revelation in azure, the great prairies and savannahs, the Arctic summer, and the warm splendour of the southern night, are all rendered on canvas by realistic painters, working with the aim of making these things visible to non-travelling children. If the teacher uses a book, it is a book full of pictures—a book written too by literary artists, each describing one place that he knows and has lived in. Such geography primers in Russia bear the names of Tolstoy, Gorky, and other master painters in words, every one of whom has lent his aid to the primary school teacher.[1]

Tolstoy himself gives us a picture of his evening class. "Come to the school in the twilight ; there is

[1] Among school suppliers Holzel of Vienna sends out sets of oleographs—copies of pictures painted for schools by the greatest landscape painters—the larger set of twenty-eight copies costing about £9, the smaller reproductions only 9s.

no light in the windows; all is peaceful. The snow
is on the stairs; there is a faint murmur, a slight
movement behind the door, a boy runs upstairs two
steps at a time, and enters the class room. It is almost dark behind the frosty panes. . . .

"It seems as if all were dead; nothing moves.
Are they not asleep? You advance in the shadow,
and examine the face of one of the smaller boys.
He is sitting, devouring the teacher with his eyes, and
his intense attention makes him frown. You tickle
his neck, he does not even smile, he shakes his head as
if to drive away a fly. He is entirely absorbed in the
mysterious story of how the veil of the temple was
rent in twain, and the sky was darkened. It is at
once painful and sweet to them."

The class is seeing pictures. The little boy who
has never been far from his own village sees the rent
curtain. He sees the sky that darkens with wrath,
not with rain.

It is the teacher who has opened his eyes—has
flung wide this new door through which so much is
visible. He devours this teacher with his eyes, and
does not see him. But he will see the vision a
thousand times. It is his for ever.

To take an English example now.

Miss Whelan, a teacher near Worthing, is founding

all her scheme of education in her school on
art—and above all on drama. The children learn
history by becoming actors and inventing *tableaux
vivants*. They choose who shall personate different
characters, they mount the stage and arrange the
scenes.[1] Geography, too, is taught after the same
method. In the *Review of Reviews* for December,
1906, we have an account of a drama-geography
lesson on Canada—some of the children dressed as
animals, some as settlers, some as Indians. Literature
also is taught by plays and pictures ; and it is said
that the dullest boys and girls wake up as if by
magic when this new way of learning is put within
their reach. It is as though light were suddenly
flashed into dark chambers. Lo! The dark chambers
are roomy and handsome enough, after all, though
wofully empty! It was long assumed that they did
not exist!

Grown-up people look for pictures in literature, in

[1] Many years ago, having despaired of creating any real interest for
history in two very intelligent little girl pupils, I began to write
historical plays for them. The first, "The Princes in the Tower,"
was acted with tremendous success before an audience of Sussex
villagers, and was printed afterwards. Flushed with joy and cheered
by the applause of the rustics, we then acted "Lady Jane Grey" and,
I think, "Jack Cade's Rebellion," but a paraffin lamp, ill fixed, fell
down, and nearly set us all on fire. So the entertainments came to
a sudden end. The villagers grieved. They had put out the fire,
and were hoping to see more history pictures.

drama, and travel, and children look for them, and will not care for things of which they have had no vision.

.   .   .   .   .   .

It was very late in its history that the race wanted eye-instruments. For ages the human eye did its work unassisted save by rude glasses that could hardly be looked upon as eye instruments. Its rich associations with touch were developed by work, and also by modelling and drawing;[1] but more remarkable than all this was the development of the vast psychic field that is the peculiar feature of human vision—the weaving of what was seen into dreams, visions, Utopias. No doubt it was well that projection was not hurried; and for the same reasons it would be well that it should not be hastened in childhood. When at last it came it was simple enough—and begun, one would say, by chance.

---

[1] It is saddening to see how the rich training of the eye afforded in free drawing is evaded. Even when good ideals are introduced, yet the methods tend continually to be debased. For example, no sooner was free-arm drawing and free design introduced than a great weight of new and expensive "apparatus," sheets of copies, with skeleton lines and coloured flower forms, were flung on the market. These are all substitutes—substitutes for the power to draw, for the courage to trust children and let them trust themselves; substitutes for helpful mistakes even—for the going wrong that helps the beginner to do better; substitutes, in fact, for *true* hand and eye training!

Nearly three hundred years ago John Battista Porta, a Neapolitan, made a hole in a wall in front of a dark room, and noticed that the rays entering, cast a shadow picture of the things outside. The hole was a projected eyeball, and the wall a choroid or curtain behind it. Gazing in wonder through this new order of eyeball, Battista Porta began to think of furnishing it, of putting something more behind it, and he put in—the first thing that he would have met if he had been examining his *own* eye—a lens! In that hour the long ages of free exercise closed. One eye-instrument maker after another appeared, and the eye unshrouded itself. One of the greatest was Galileo, a doctor, who was not only a great projector of the eye, but was the first projector of the pulse in the clock or timepiece.[1] "He took an old small organ pipe, jammed a spectacle-glass into either end, and behold! a magnifying glass!" Crowds

---

[1] In one of his books Oliver Lodge tells how Galileo, praying one day in the Cathedral like a good Catholic, as he was all his life, saw a great lamp swinging to and fro after the verger had lighted it; and how he (Galileo) began to time the swings by the only watch he possessed—his own pulse; how he noticed that the time of swing remained, as near as he could tell, the same, though the swings were getting smaller; and how he thus discovered the law on which the pendulum and all modern clocks are based. Galileo was at that time a doctor, and wanted to count people's pulses, and the pendulum served, just as watches (or pulsologies, as the first watches were called) still serve all doctors for the same purpose.

of people gazed through it, and Galileo went on grinding new lenses—making rude telescopes (such as children might still make and use—could be led on to make spontaneously to-day). From that time the eye-projecting instrument makers multiplied in many lands, and at last from the nation of all others whe *see* quickly and clearly[1] (that is, the French) a man arose—Daguerre—who projected the eye so fully that every book on elementary physiology describes the eye by describing his invention, the photographic camera.

Even if the question is considered in detail, and the very latest discoveries with regard to the life taken into account, the fact of projection is driven home. We will cite one out of many. Photographers found that light will break up iodide of silver, and that with the aid of iodide of silver, therefore, they could get negatives ; but nature had got negatives by the action of light on eye pigment for æons. Many years after the silver salts began to be used in photography—in 1876—Ball found that light breaks

[1] Thus, as Galton points out, the French are the nation who can speak and write clearly, even where other nations speak and write obscurely. In their scientific books all is clear as daylight. In their poems there is a kind of sharpness of outline that destroys the artistic effect. And their language is full of expressions such as "On voit clair," or "Ca se voit," or "Figurez vous ça?"

H

up the coloured substance in the retina of the eye. He experimented with mice-eyes—kept the mice in a darkened room, then exposed them suddenly in face of objects in a strong light. Then he destroyed the mice and examined the eyes. There he found optograms of the things they had last gazed at printed off like negatives—or rather they formed original negatives in the optogram, or eye photograph.

Within the seeker or worker there is something that always awaits the inventor when he reaches the goal. The *really* original thing in him is something that was gained in the free period when he used his powers as a child, as a primitive man, and also as an artist.

From all this it appears first that instruments, like tools, should not be made very early in life.

And also that when a boy or girl really begins to require instruments, he or she should make them *himself* or *herself*—make, that is to say, rude and simple instruments, which are true projections; should grind his own lenses, when he needs eye-instruments, like Galileo or Herschel, and make the tools he needs like Newton. This seems to be the order of progression followed by the race, and no doubt it will be followed by the individual long after we have ceased to look for "norms" of work in any system, even in systems that bear such names as Froebel and Solomon (the father of sloyd).[1]

[1] This does not mean, of course, that a child should not look through a modern microscope or telescope. There is no reason why he should not have the vision made possible by them, any more than there is a reason why he should not see Holzel's wonderful picture of the Sahara or the Rockies. The vision feeds the imagination, and that is the thing that cannot be done too soon, as the child himself proves by his eagerness to look at and hold the pictures !

And yet the looking at far-off things and through microscopes does not take the place of that outward movement—the self-projection that seems to be as necessary for human growth as is breathing, or simple movement.

CHAPTER VII

THE PROJECTION OF MOVEMENT, OR MOTOR POWER

WE come now to the projection, not of a hand merely, or even of a fist, but of muscle and movement.

Certainly the fist will not be forgotten! At Krupp's works in Essen there is a hammer head that could literally crush a mountain. There are iron arms to-day that can laugh at storms, steel hands that can tear the rocks. The originals of these were not very powerful, and yet there is nothing so hard and unyielding that they cannot rend it. And they can thread a hair and sheer an invisible thread. How did all this begin?

It began long ago, for long ago people must have wanted, not only to strike, cut, and carry, but also to lift and to draw.

They wanted levers.

So we have now to consider a kind of projection that has gone on for ages, and then after ages halted, and finally in modern days appeared to find a soul and to develop in a way that must either lift us up into a higher kind of life or destroy us for ever.

Every school boy knows that there are three kinds of levers in the body. The first is that in which the moving point is between the power and the weight —as, for example in the head, or rather in the skull, which is placed so that the face can be raised freely at one end, and the back of the head at another. Among levers of this order are the see-saw, the balance and some kinds of crowbar, and many examples of this kind of lever are, as we should expect, to be found in very old mechanisms—such as the " shadoof"—a pillar of Nile mud with a swing beam and a bucket which a man dipped into the water. A lever of the second order is to be found in the lifted foot, and its projection in the homely wheelbarrow or in a crowbar when used for lifting a weight while one of its ends rests on the ground.

There is yet one other order of lever which may be studied in the lifting of the forearm, in the straightening of a limb after bending, and in the treadle of a machine. All these were projected long ago. But the body did not yield up all its secrets—and will never do so, since it is always creating a new mystery.

What is the ideal for all kinds of moving things? It is to have a perfect power of stopping or controlling the movement. That is true in all work—and in conduct. It is true in mechanics and in morals. In work it was for ages the hand that was the great controlling agent—and almost the only one. But the hand cannot be in many places at once. It cannot be active and controlling many things at once. And so the power of man, though very beautiful in work, was also very restricted. It was also very uncertain. This did not matter so much when one was dealing with inert things, with wood that lay still on the bench, and metals that were under the power of the moulder every moment. But when motor power itself was projected, it was a very different matter. To give oneself up to the mercy of steam is not a thing that even the most confiding would care to do.

Our fathers did not give themselves up entirely even to wind and tide. At first, as we have seen, they were so wary of the sea that they went afloat only in fair weather. Later they coaxed it, as it were, with sail and oar. The miller, too, risking less, took favours from wind and wave, and was thankful. That was the age of complete force-closure, as it is called in mechanics—an age when humanity still looked on the forces of nature, as powerful and helpful, but when it was still quite helpless to guide or control them to any great extent for its own purposes.

However, there was in the muscular system even of the human body something very different to this system of "laissez-faire." "After a bone has been moved by a muscle," says the elementary physiology book, "it is brought back to its former position by the action of a second muscle on its opposite side." Hence we find that muscles are generally arranged in pairs, each muscle of a pair being antagonistic in its action to the other. Rouleaux, the great authority on mechanics, says that the present day ideal of the great mechanic is to advance *from force-closure to pair-closure.* In force-closure, as we have seen, the forces of nature are used to stop some movement of a machine, but in pair-closure the machine itself can stop itself—like a moral person! The ideal of the mechanic, as well as of the saint, is self-control.

This ideal then which is being slowly realized by the mechanic, and more slowly yet by all civilized men in the moral sphere, had yet been for ages illustrated in every part of the muscular system.

Why (since it is the open secret of the muscular system) was not this ideal realized quickly in machinery? All kinds of reasons may be given, but there is one that seems to deserve a good deal of respect. It is the fact that for ages labour had been despised, and the labourer degraded, to be a mere chattel of others, not *his own man*. Charles Ham recalls this fact very often, and every one who writes on education through work recalls it. For at every point he is reminded of it as of a blight that destroyed a great seed field. "For ages," said Horace Mann (whom Ham quotes), "the labour of the world has been done by ignorant men—by classes doomed to ignorance from sire to son—by the bondsmen and bondswomen of the Jews, by the helots of Sparta, by the villeins and slaves of modern times. . . ." These were never free men in any real sense, and so their power halted at the projection of mere limbs and organs. It halted before it reached the projection of vital function, before it reached the outskirts of the kingdom of will—that is, motive power and all its possibilities. It was a pretty halting place, and a safe one. The workers strewed it with flowers. They decked it with ornament. It is wonderful to see the delicacy of the work—also its radiance, its beauty and exuberance. It is the work of a glad and gifted child free in a garden, bathed in morning light, sweet with the perfume of young flowers and holding still the hush of dawn! *Such* work should be done in all elementary schools.

For it is the gift of morning—the work of childhood. How free it seems, as well as lovely—and how irresponsible! But this is the freedom of children, not of men and women. One may fall in love with such freedom, but one should not be content with it too long, on pain of becoming grown-up children—that is, semi-slaves. For though Ruskin said that these craftsmen of yesterday were more than the factory hand of to-day, because they were free to do beautiful work, that is not *all* the truth. It is true the hand was free to project itself; but not the muscles—else the hammer of a Thor might have fallen on the master.

The serf age ended when the workman, ignorant as he was, began to project the muscular system freely. It was then that the new era began (after a long halt) in the workshops of England.

The history of that awakening is, in reality, the history of modern England. All the political struggles of the last two hundred years are a part of the travail through which the genius of the race gave birth to a new order of life, and carried self-realization through work into an entirely new field. Henceforward it reproduced life, *not in forms merely,*

but in forces. It did not simply mould the inert.
It gave it a kind of soul, a soul hardly more relent-
less than its own primitive soul, and harnessed and
held it with brake and counter forces. The men
who did all this were not learned men. They were
not the heads of colleges, nor did they hold degrees.
One cannot say that they were more than vigorous
workmen, whose vigour and eager life, stimulated
by labour, demanded new tools. It was they who
struck off the fetters of feudalism. Watt, the
instrument maker, Stephenson the brakesman,
Telford the mason, Rennie the wheelwright, Dudley
the artisan, Brindley, and Cartwright, and a host of
other practical men, made the great projections,
which were, among other things, *an enfranchisement*
(in some small degree at least) *of the human will.*
Their work well begun, the whole problem of human
existence presented itself in a new light. The
gaiety and radiance of dawn fled suddenly, and the
world grew stern. The light was hidden by murky
clouds, and the land was even black and lurid in
large districts. The fear of hunger was like a lash
to myriads. Yet the people had broken loose from
their masters, and had to fight now only for further
self-emancipation.

What is holding them back? A great many things

still hamper them, but there is one above all others
that hugs more closely at their straining arms than
any other, and that is the fact that *our educational
system is far in the rear of the Spirit of the New Age.*
It is timid. It is timid as the ancient Greeks who
hugged the coast in stormy times. It is afraid to let
youth project freely. Yet the question begins to
define itself, and to be asked more boldly—

"Should boyhood halt just where the race halted
for ages?" Woodwork centres are opened ; ironwork
centres even are opened. That is very well. But is
that all? As children grow older they put away
childish things, but their impulsion is still reliable.
They cease to want to become a humble order of
artisan. Most of the boys want to be engineers!

And meantime thousands of mere machine-minders
are being turned away. And there is a greater demand for skilled and inventive workers in the *real*
workshops of the future!

It is not for the school doctor—camping hastily as
it were on the outskirts of school life—to enter yet
on a full explanation and justification of this new
impulse of youth. He has had but little chance for
studying it—a new arrival as he is, and still looked
upon, by many, as a mere notifier of infectious
diseases. Yet this is part of his work. What is

more, nothing is safe till this has been done. Many reforms have been carried already, and lost for lack of it. Some reforms are, indeed, always in jeopardy till science has put their value beyond dispute. People will find substitutes for them—or what they regard as substitutes. The moralist may declare he should have lessons on temperance, truthfulness, diligence, and a score of other virtues (which may be true enough). But lessons do not take the place of life. Some may expect the school doctor to confine himself to showing methods by which the boys can escape having favus, or eye-diseases. But the greater service will have been rendered only when he brings reasons to show how or why the education the youth once longed for (or would, in any case, have eagerly responded to) would have saved him from moral and physical shipwreck. The new technical schools already show that this education saves —they show, at least, pupils who, at first feeble and unstable of character, after a certain time become strong, and self-controlled, and are saved from shipwreck. But the schools where such training is given are in peril all the time. Who will believe their report? It is still only a report. The thing that would give it authority is still lacking. The men who could find out and explain why this is so do not even so much as get a chance to consider it.   So the discovery of the new order of schools is at the mercy of every wind that blows.   It is no more ours than is the bird who alights on the window-sill, and who then, startled by her own arrival, flies away before we welcome her.

But now a word of these new ventures—the schools themselves.

The pioneer one was founded, it appears, in Moscow, in 1868, by Dellavos.   Prince Kropotkin gives some account of its methods in his *Fields, Factories, and Workshops*.   It was a school quite in the ordinary sense of the word, taking in boys at the age of fourteen, after an examination such as is represented by our "leaving certificate."   Only *this* school became a real industrial centre at the top.   It merged into a genuine part of the industrial and financial world.   The boys were "finished" by becoming *bona fide* wage-earners, competing in the open market with highly skilled workmen, making with their own hands "electric machines, steam engines (from the heavy boiler to the last finely turned screw), agricultural machinery, and scientific apparatus."

Just as the youth at Oxford tests himself by speaking and writing in public, the youth of the

Moscow school went through a much more searching kind of test—a test that surely will appeal to all truly manly youths and practical men. They passed from the class room to the open market, and took their final examination, not under the eyes of mere inspectors, but in the real world—the open seas of industrial life. Yet in full view of the teacher!

The school at Moscow was destroyed, but others have followed its lead. Kropotkin mentions, for example, Gordon's College, Aberdeen, and there are others. The technical school at Chicago which took Dellavos' school avowedly as its model was started through the generosity of a few rich men in the seventies, and Charles Ham, in his book *Manual Training*, gives a full account of its work.

There is nothing strange or novel about it—and yet it is bold. At every stage the pupil resumes all he has learned from the first lesson, and then goes forward unflinchingly—recapitulating the industrial life of the world. Drawing is the basis of the work at every stage, so the pupils spend a great deal of time over this subject. But the work is related to history, and even physical geography in the earlier stages. The pupils enter the carpenter's shop, and there they make in wood the patterns they will make later in metal. (Some of these American boys have been brought up in the backwoods, and the teacher, at this stage, turns aside to hear their impressions and talk of trees. Their fresh bright talk of the virgin forest and its wonders arrests the casual reader, but it will be matched in England perhaps one day, when geography is taught out of doors.) Then they go into the wood-turner's shop, and there they are introduced to steam-driven machinery of whose power they are warned : " Death lurks in the shafts and pulleys." Work is certainly not play here. The pupils manage edged tools driven by machinery. *Ernst is das Leben*—revolutions are not made with rose water.   Neither are men made by handling toys and making verses.   The new education is much more tender than the old—but it is also a great deal more stern and grave.   Its tenderness is real, and it is safeguarded by knowledge ; its sternness is not in the mien of a teacher, but in the nature of the things to which the pupil has access.   Thus the early education (with its care of the body) generates power, but power can continue to be generated only through the exercise of what has already come into existence.   The pupil passes from the metal work to the forging room.   At every step the work grows more grave, more absorbing.   It is, as we

said, not the teacher who grows stern, but the work.
We are told that the pupil gains as much power in a
day in the school forge as he would gain in a year in
an ordinary smith's shop.

Finally the step is taken that makes the child who
for fifteen years has haunted the world of the past,
unconscious of its shades, a denizen of the modern
world.   The pupils go into the machine tool laboratory.   They are now from 17 to 20 years old.   They
have to resume all they have learned in science, in
art, in ethics : working as *modern*, up-to-date artisans.
The graduating test is significant.   They do not sit
down to examination papers or answer surprising
questions.   They make " a project."   Language has
grown frank at last—gone back to origins.   Each
pupil makes his own project, a complete engine, a
steam pump, an electric machine.   He makes every
part of it, and when it is done he watches it tremble
as if awakening from sleep, " watches the shaft
oscillate slowly, then faster, then regularly like a
strong heart-pulse."   And in the emotion shown
by even the oldest of these very cool, disciplined
young workmen we get a revelation at last surely of
the fact that the growing realization of part of the
organism is necessary for the evolution of the higher
life.   One is held back as with bands till this is

done. But when it is done the worker is set free in some new way. What the whole meaning of this deliverance may be we cannot say. Our school doctors have not told us yet.

Two things, however, strike one very forcibly in regard to these pupils of the new order of schools.

We have seen that the health of the message-boys and child wage-earners fails suddenly, in a way that cannot be accounted for entirely by mere hardship or hunger.

We also saw that they lost ambition.

Well, the pupils of the Technical College of Chicago, and similar schools, were remarkable, first, because of their splendid physique at the end of the course.

And secondly, because of the great and growing ambition of every pupil.

Of the boys in the forging room Ham says: "They are manly-looking, animated, erect, and show the pride of conscious strength." In the smithy "their faces are aglow with the flush of health. . . ." Of the young men in the machine tool shop: "They are now from seventeen to twenty years old. They are robust, hearty-looking. Their bearing is very resolute. Their attitude erect. They are full-chested, muscular-armed."

I

So much for the physique.   Now for the other great "result."

The ambition of the educated mechanic is a thing by itself, and is not to be confounded with the ambition of even the highest order of literary man.   It is quite as ardent, but it is a great deal more confident. This enthusiasm and ambition effervesces in even the younger artisan boys.   They are all going to make improvements and inventions, and they know of a score that require to be made, and that they may very well take a part in.   As a matter of fact the young mechanic's ambitions are quite reasonable. There is no other field of invention where *so many* may make useful contributions ; and the pupils know this.

Each knows that by working hard he may do some very important thing—that he may improve a machine, discover an improved way of dyeing, forging, tempering, a new way of applying what he has learned. Compare this with the ambition of the poet, the artist, the politician, the orator, so vague, troubled. . . . It is not, perhaps, a higher ambition.   It may appear at the first blush a humbler one ; but it is more impersonal. It makes less appeal to vanity and egoistic desires. The desire for "fame" plays but a small part in it.   The incentives to vanity are not quickened in dealing, as the artisan deals, with the forces of nature—they are quelled rather. They are quelled even in handwork. The finest mechanics of the past got little credit for their work. The man who made the sword Excalibur was not immortalized, though the sword was immortalized. No doubt some great hand workers suffered through neglect, and wished for recognition. What is more remarkable, however, is that they seem to have suffered infinitely less through such causes than did other orders of great men. Our great inventors, too, so little talked about even to-day, suffer less ; and this detachedness appears even in the fully-trained pupils of the new technical college. " It may be," said Ham, "that there are vain statesmen, kings, priests, but we should as little expect to find a vain mechanic as a vain scientist." That is to say, the mechanic is, morally, in some respects at least, the higher order of person.

But this elevation of one kind of worker is not due certainly to any innate superiority ; *it is more probably the result of the training given in his work.* This integral kind of technical training extends beyond childhood into youth ; and it seems to favour in these stormy years the harmonious working of *many* awakening brain centres.

.   .   .   .   .   .

One cannot here attempt the task of showing what youth is. This is no place for it. The psychology of youth is in its infancy. True, the foundation is being laid by such men as Stanley Hall (in his book *Adolescence*) and by others. But the study of the adolescent is new. The existence of the elementary school has made it almost necessary to carry on the study of early childhood and to get to know something about the child. But the existence of adult schools, evening classes and technical schools, does not seem to have made it so clear that there is something to learn about youth as well as about childhood. Most people who consider evening schools or training colleges even, do so from the point of view of critics, not students, and so it happens that few are on really safe ground when they are dealing with the hobble-dehoy of either sex. A word or two is all we can say here.

The adolescent, or girl or boy between thirteen and twenty-one is living through a period of rapid growth and great physical development. How great and rapid this change is we may judge from the great increase in the weight of the various organs, but more especially of the heart. Between the ages of fourteen and eighteen the child appears indeed to be passing into

THE PROJECTION OF MOVEMENT 117

a new house, into a kind of dwelling which is strange
to him, and of which he is hardly the master. That
is why he is awkward, embarrassed by the sudden
growth, for example of the lower limbs, which
made people invent for him the name of hobble-
dehoy. The effects of this sudden impulse of
growth are not only interesting, but very various.
It may break up old barriers like a storm, so that a
boy or girl who appeared in childhood very defective
may come suddenly into a new heritage, and appear
henceforth as normal or almost normal. The
affections as well as the intellect usually suddenly
expand and deepen in a very remarkable way,
that seems to transform the character. On the
other hand, this is an age when all kinds of here-
ditary defects and weaknesses declare themselves.
Criminologists testify that the great majority of
people become criminals between the ages of
sixteen and twenty-three. In adolescence a great
proportion of all suicides take place ; the hold on
life is less tenacious than it will be later, when, perhaps, life will have lost its charms. Deeds of heroism
are common in adolescence, and one has not to read
history in order to see how often youths and maidens
have led or served forlorn causes. The philosopher
is nearly always old : the hero is nearly always

young.   But whether it be heroism or criminality that youth brings in its train, this phase of life is always one of stress and storm, of eruption, and of revelation.   The organism then as it were shows its hand.   It is exposed through the turmoil of rapid growth, and, like the sea in tempest, yields up its secrets.

Imagination, which is the motor power in mind, is of course dominant during this period.   It is more uncontrolled if not more creative than it will ever be again.   Even those who will never again be artists are artists in youth.   Youths and girls hide verses they have written away, distrusting quite rightly the instinct of the older person on finding them.[1]   And as even the most original imagination requires at first a guide or master, so every adolescent is at first a disciple.   A popular orator or public person holds the imagination of many young people in secret for years, while the ideal of the parent, which may be a higher one in a sense, does not probably in the least attract them.   The parent's ideal as a rule is rational, beyond the point where it remains lovely in the eyes of youth.   As a rule, indeed, it is only the noblest elements in it that even feebly attract youth.

[1] The Germans have a word for this kind of literature—"Schwär-merei."

It is quite clear, then, that youth has a great deal to lose as well as to gain, and it is a consciousness of this that inspired such phrases as "Whom the gods love die young" and "Be true to the dreams of thy youth."

The working-class boy of fourteen who goes to the mill has some difficulty in keeping his dream. He has difficulty in even conceiving the dream of youth at all or embodying it in any form at all. But the lad or girl who receives a merely scrappy and pseudo literary training, or who is taught science from text-books without applying anything learned, is not in a much better case. Experience comes to him, but it is for the most part experience of people whose growth is arrested like his own, and dealing with them he learns only a kind of worldly wisdom and a contempt for his young dream ! Maturity, as well as age, brings thus merely a kind of degeneration.[1]

But for the new technical training we may claim that it favours a movement that is not degenerative in any sense, but progressive. All through the rationalizing process goes on and is not checked.

[1] Of the noisy, violent behaviour of these in holiday times we have spoken already. That is a more elementary kind of expansion than the Schwärmerei of the sentimental German school girl or boy, but it is, if carried far, an indication of lack—not of natural power, but of opportunities for its expression.

It consists, not in the discovery of the perversions
of human beings, but in the discovery of the nature
of materials and the forces of nature and of what
is possible in dealing with them.   Thus the development of reason is accompanied by no inner blight
or withering.   It does not bring in its train loss
of faith or weakening of sympathies.   Rather it
strengthens faith, not in self or in some showy public
character, or even in one great inventor, but in a
great army of nameless inventors and workers—in
humanity.   And the worker's imagination is not
weakened.   It is exercised in new ways, and em-
braces realities more completely and truly.   He
is not held in a slavish, half-hypnotic trance.
Obscurely perhaps, but more and more strongly, he
feels the rallying and renewal of life within him,
advancing without pause or arrest towards some
new goal.

Of course all this is not demonstrated quite
clearly yet.   There are too few of the new order of
schools and writers[1] to warrant us in speaking
with authority.   But those who have come into

---

[1] " The psychology of the artist " has been dealt with by Arreaé and
others.   The psychology of the artisan waits its exponent.   Perhaps a
school doctor will write it one day.   But already it seems safe, however,
to say that it will be the story of a healthy brain, whose development
extends at least to the verge of manhood.

existence all give the same kind of testimony. They testify that of all the non-selected pupils received, none have turned out badly. And it is shown on the other hand that among the wrecks of society there are hardly any who have had even the beginnings of this kind of education.

CHAPTER VIII

THE PROJECTION OF NERVES

HERE we may halt—in a book about children. But a glance forward and beyond them may be allowed. What we may call the projection of nerves has taken place very rapidly—all within the last century and a half.

As always happens, the artisan inventor was ahead of the physiologist and discoverer. (Sometimes, of course, the inventor *becomes* the discoverer.) In 1774, Le Sage laid insulated metal wires under the Rhine and connected these with pith-ball electroscopes. There were twenty-four wires, one for each letter of the alphabet, and the message was transmitted by frictional electricity. This was sixty years or more before Dubois Raymond begun his studies on nerve fibre—that is, on nervous conductors of the body. But even in the early telegraphs the wire reproduced the fibre more or less in detail, having gaps in the supports, as in the fibre, and reproducing too the outer sheath. And every year saw a host of seekers and experimenters arise, all on the track of a secret, the key to which was within. And at last the modern industrial world began to have a nervous system.

So fast and free the messages began to thrill along those new fibres that the wit of the inventor was taxed to find ways of transmitting messages from wire to wire, of sending more than one message through one wire, of sending many currents indeed along every wire in a second. Speed is not only a test of fitness—it is one of the *great* tests in so far as the nervous system is concerned,[1] and it is the great test of telegraph systems. And now, one and another inventor vied with one another, tripped one another up almost, in the perfecting of the apparatus for rapid transmission. One can read the story of how they brought out " combiners," " receivers," and " distributers," and how they learned to utilize all the delivery capacity of their wire, in any popular work on modern telegraphy. It is a dizzy chapter in the story of human history. And it seems, at first, as if nothing in any *former* chapter prepared us at all to read *this* one.

---

[1] This is so true that intelligence is tested by speed, and doctors speak of backward and defective children often as " children of slow response."

The year 1860 was memorable, for it was in this year that M. Rouvier published his scheme of "multiple transmission." In 1860, too, Broca, the pioneer of the physiology of the brain, proved that certain speech defects are associated with disease of a small part of the brain in the third left frontal convolution, and showed how different areas have special functions and receive a particular kind of message. He was, no doubt, very far from dreaming *how* complicated and diverse as a receiving medium the human brain is, but he was able to localize the function of speech, and thus to lay the foundation of all that made it possible for us to learn something about the hitherto unknown world of the cerebral cortex.

What connexion had this event with the other? That is to say, with the rapid development of a telegraphic system over the world? It appears to have had a certain connexion. For many years Broca worked, and before him men like him, Dubois Raymond, and other physiologists, were studying the nerve fibre, the electric action of nerves and muscle, and the transmission of nerve excitement. They found that there are hundreds of miles of nerve fibre in the human body, and that this fibre in living beings is just as much a roadway for traffic as is any line or cable ever laid. "Suppose," says an admirer

of Dubois Raymond, "that the nerves of hearing
and of sight of a man were cut, and the outer end of
the former was perfectly joined to the central end
of the latter, then the sound of an orchestra would
awaken in us the sensation of light and colour, and
if the fibre serving the centre of vision was affixed
to the hearing part of the brain, then a highly
coloured picture would give us impressions of
sound!" Thus far, in function as well as form, the
parallelism between fibre and wire is as close as
it well could be.

However, physiologists and artisans worked apart
as usual. For years the latter made efforts to lay
a cable between America and England. Once and
again they set forth to make the attempt. Every
one knows how they failed again and again, and how
fruitful these failures were ; how they indicated to
Sir William Thomson a means of helping the baffled
workers by improving the receiving centre by his
new sensitive galvanometer. They made the fibre—
he made the brain cells. And then at last, in 1860,
across the wild ocean lifting its steep, blue, moving
hills for thousands of leagues the fibre was laid that
joined two continents.

Over the leaf is a drawing (from Ernest Kapp's book)
of transverse cuttings of cable, and of nerve fibre. On

looking at the former alone, one might feel tempted to say " How could they think of it ? " But on glancing at the fibre, this wonder gives place to another, and

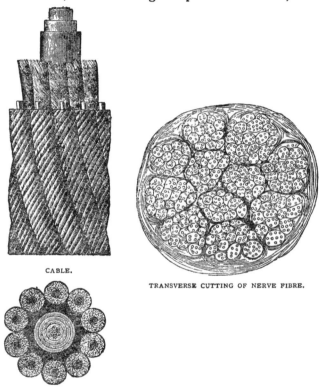

CABLE.

TRANSVERSE CUTTING OF NERVE FIBRE.

TRANSVERSE CUTTING OF CABLE.

we may say rather, " Nothing do we think. *It thinks in us."*

Many of the great writers of the nineteenth

century hated machinery with a personal hatred. The chief of these was Ruskin, who can hardly mention it without scorn. The idealism of William Morris was expressed largely in crafstmanship as opposed to machine-made things. Carlyle did not extend his lectures on heroes so as to include the artisan. He ended with the hero as poet and as man of letters, thus far and no further! He often makes comparisons between men and machines, and even trees and machines, greatly to the disadvantage of the latter. For example, "O, that we could displace the machine god and put a man god in his place!" and "I find no similitude of life so true as this of a tree! Beautiful! Machine of the universe! Do but think of that in contrast!"

But it was reserved for the workers themselves to hate machinery in earnest—not in word only, but in deed. A machine is never perhaps quite a soulless thing to the person who works it, or who has made it (that is perhaps why the engine-driver alludes to his engine as " her " not " it," and why the sailor speaks of his vessel as if it were a woman). And when in the eighteenth century a half-mad boy smashed a machine because it seemed to rob him or hurt him, the learned felt pity, but the workers felt sympathy. They came to hate machinery with a personal hatred, and to forget the makers of it in their hatred. Through books, out of print now and forgotten, one can get a glimpse of these poor men, confused by the power of this new factor in industry, and maddened by hunger. One reads for example how to an old mill in a lovely Yorkshire valley came a party of workmen one wild night in March—how, armed with crowbars, bludgeons, and hammers, they pushed open the door of the engine-room and gazed in. By fitful moonlight they could see the engine—the foe that had taken the food from their children's lips. It was still now. Its cruel soul slept. They gazed half-stupefied, half-fascinated. Then they fell on the monster and hacked it to pieces. When a force of armed men, representing the owners and masters, came over the hill in the morning they did not even think of showing fight to them, still less of showing fear. They set off for another mill—there to hack and maim another machine.

The impulse was blind of course, but the presentiment of the machine-breakers was only too true. Machinery increased productive power enormously, but its effect on the children of the factory people and working population was not very favourable![1]

---

[1] And this has become more than ever apparent, thanks to the labours of the school doctor. Take for example this Chart, transcribed by Charles Roberts, F.R.C.S., showing the actual relative heights of boys

The explosions of rage and despair with which one new machine after another was succeeded became

of the ages of eleven and twelve in the year 1873 as compared with Dr. Arkell's in 1907.

Height in inches.	Public Schools, Country.	Middle Lower Class.	Factories.	Industrial.
60				
59				
58	Mean height.			
57				
55	55 inches.			
54		54 inches.		
53				
52			52 inches.	
51				
50				50 inches.
49				
48				

Dr. Arkell's Chart for 1907 :—

Mean Height of boys of eleven at Secondary Schools 55·5 inches.

Children of middle and lower middle

Class A.	53·1 inches.
Factory hand Class B. . .	51·8 inches.
Industrial school Class C. .	49·7 inches.

From Dr. Roberts' Table of Weights in 1873 for boys of eleven of Factory hand class 67·7 lb :—

Mean weight of boys in 1907 at eleven from Dr. Arkell's chart.

Secondary School	70 lb.
Children of Middle and Lower Middle Class . .	61·4 lb.
Factory Class	59 lb.
Industrial School Class	55·5 lb.

Thus it would appear that the eleven year old child of that very large class of workers who are in regular employment but with small wages has lost in the past thirty years more than 8 lb. in weight, and this serious loss has taken place in spite of the great advance in medical science and the improved sanitation of cities. Thus, the rapid improvement in machinery cannot be said to have brought any very great benefit to them.

K

feebler of course in time. The people resigned themselves, and began to feel, above all, that this progressive movement which did not favour them was in the nature of things and inevitable. Steam-power was like a brute-soul. It devoured the young, dismissed the old, and degraded the adult so that he became the rival, as wage-slave, of his wife and child. Under the black pall of the mill-smoke these gloomy thoughts formed and wandered through the vacant minds of myriads.

But the movement that made modern industrial Britain—the projection of the moving power itself and all its organs—did not hesitate, because of the hardships it brought on innocent lives. It paused no more for these causes than does a blizzard or a north wind. It swept on. It swept past, or rather is sweeping past. And now electricity is beginning to displace steam as a motor power.

And electricity has had a different kind of first greeting. No one is angry with it. Everyone is amazed at it. After every new and startling discovery, such as that of the Becquerel Rays, the Röntgen Rays, etc., the public seems to hold its breath, to listen with mystification, with awe, and to expect it knows not what. More than one scientist has remarked this love of mystery that makes many people welcome the very latest discoveries in physics as the people centuries ago would have hailed "miracles" and "signs." But its effect on the workers was reassuring. "This great power should not pass into the hands of the few," said one of their representatives the other day. "It should become the instrument of the people, and not of a ruling class."

One cannot but dwell with pleasure on the fact that electric cables, and wires, and "installations" of every kind are projections, not of fighting organs, like the common knife or hammer, but of the nervous system. The nervous system which drains *feeling*, as it were, from every region of the body, collects it in special organs, attracts it, as Luys says, by means of nervous conductors, so that it becomes a mobile force, transmissible to a distance: the nervous system, which makes sympathy and unity possible! It has got itself projected at last! And just as light, though terrible, is reassuring, so those projections that bind continents together, and make the lonely station a part of the busy world, are chasing away the last terrors of the dark ages, wiping out their dark dreams.

Yes! that same energy which makes communication between people thousands of miles apart possible, and destroys distance, is not only present in

us, but through it we move, and live, and have our
being. Through it we move (because muscles, above
all other tissues of the body, except nerves, exercise
electric action). Through it we live, for what life is
possible without electricity? And as for the human
Brain itself, it not only exercises such action, it
appears to offer the original of all conductors, co-
herers, multipliers, condensers, transmitters, and all
other electrical apparatus whatsoever, and to make
life of a higher kind possible through these. Long
years have passed since Dubois Raymond began the
serious study of the electric phenomena of nerves,
muscles, and glands; long years have passed since
he showed by experiment that the magnetic current
can be deflected by the Will.[1] And now, though large
areas of the brain hold their secrets fast-locked, yet
the middle or motor brain has yielded up its secret.

[1] Rosenthal thus describes the experiment. "The ends of the wire
of the multiplier were connected with two vessels filled with liquid,
and the index finger of both hands dipped in these vessels. A rod
arranged in front of the vessel served to steady the position of the
hands. Currents are then present in the muscles of both arms and of
the breast, which, since the groups of muscles are symmetrically
arranged, cancel each other, acting one on the other. When all is
thus arranged, the man strongly contracts the muscle of one arm; the
result is an immediate deflection of the multiplier, which indicates the
presence of a current ascending in the contracted arm from the hand
to the shoulder. We are therefore able, by the mere power of the
will, to generate an electric current, and to set the magnetic needle in
motion."

And what is that great secret? Simply that its activity is electric in its nature. So true is this that, if stimulated by a current from the outside, it will, at different points, perform its functions of moving hand, lip, eye, or other member. It is demonstrably an electrical apparatus. It is also well established that the fibres of nerve-cells connect to make thinking possible—that the electric current is turned off and on constantly within us. In short, it is known that fibre and brain are the great originals of the latest order of apparatus for communication. But those whom we may still call the tool-makers of the world do not wait for indications from the brain specialist! They are forging far ahead, making "tools" for which the brain itself is not absolutely known to offer any prototype. They were on the untrodden path already, even in the days of Dubois Raymond. For, in 1838, Steinheil was dreaming of wireless telegraphy. Even then he began to show "how an indication having no connexion with the multiplier generates currents in that multiplier through the excitation of the ground above." Yet ten years ago most people were doubtful about the success of telegraphy without wires. They were doubtful; but very quickly, at last, the success of wireless telegraphy was assured, and already it is a thing grown familiar, almost commonplace. The man in the street has grown used to the idea of ether waves that are received after a journey of thousands of miles, having been guided on their journey.

True, the physiologist is again on the track of the inventor, finding new parallels in the light of the new projection. Luys and others show how the action of nerve cells resembles that of the particles in a coherer and de-coherer of a Marconi instrument, and Mr. Collins confirms this, saying that the human body " has every essential for communication at a distance, without the aid of any mechanical instruments." And this declaration was one which might be expected if precedent counts for anything. For hitherto at least work, or rather tools, have already held a prophecy. They have always foreshadowed the next great discovery as to the nature and functioning of bodily organs. If there is not every essential in the body for communication at a distance without the aid of any mechanical instruments, then something quite novel has happened. The workers have invented in a new fashion. They have taken flight, as it were, without any impetus from within.

Certainly it is no part of our task in this book to discuss such precedents and possibilities. They lie far beyond the scope of the work—beyond and outside it. Still at the threshold of the whole subject of education as the world of to-morrow will understand it, we have no call to attempt the making plain of higher problems of brain capacity and function. Happy if we can begin to set our house in order, to clear away the mass of corruption and foulness at the threshold, stem back the tide of disease and death, and establish the first principles of the hygiene of instruction—happy if we can now freely attempt this ; we need not wish to claim the right to do more.

Only we may insist that education must give free play to the impulse for progressive self-projection— that school-life must not hinder this movement, on pain of hindering all healthy development whatsoever. To-day, when the newest tools do not simply repro- duce the human hand, but the hand of genius, when the latest mechanisms show how projection is being carried ever farther into the more hidden and mys- terious recesses of the nervous structure, it is surely clear that any education, worthy the name, is a process that helps and assures free projection even in child- hood. First it aids in the projection of a rude hand ; but later, as the impulse grows and is not checked but guided, the inner life asserts itself. It follows the long track of history, cleaves it like a wing, reveals itself in the older boy's interest in mechanisms, his willingness even to endure drudgery if he may go on to the making of these.

More urgent, too, grows the vision of beautiful things gained through drama, books, drawings, and life. These strive to come forth, as it were. They feed the impulse that will project them. It is clear that this is a natural process. It is also clear that success and progress depends largely from the first on the health and vigour of bodily organs. Now these are weakened by disease. They are weakened, too, by systems of training or teaching that ignore the final aim of self-projection.

"But," it may be argued, "the majority of people must always be hewers of wood and drawers of water. They must be 'hands' always. They must serve machines, not make 'projects.'" This prophecy is really only a tradition. In every department of life science is making possible a new economy—a mode of dealing even with debris and refuse that makes these valuable as raw material.

It is not likely, then, that the greatest wealth of all, human brain power, will be dammed back and cast under for ever. Sooner or later the time must come when such a course must be looked upon as a kind of race mutilation. When the depressing influences of dirt and disease have been swept away, the race, stimulated by the nature of the discoveries with which it is surrounded, must revolt against the artificial barrier that holds back its energies. When that day comes the nature of the school doctor's task will reveal itself, and its real scope and meaning will become clear. He will no longer merely fight the battle with disease. He will safeguard nascent faculty, and declare the sacredness of growing human life, of becoming life, just as of old the religious teachers proclaimed the sacredness of mere human existence.

CHAPTER IX

THE HYGIENE OF INSTRUCTION

THAT there *is* a hygiene of instruction we have learned mainly through having given instruction that made children ill.

In some cases the children were ill already. Then the instruction was not stopped. On the contrary, it went on all the same, and ended usually in a breakdown.

The school grant did not always fail in these cases. It was found at last that 52 per cent of all the children in one city had swollen tonsils; but they all sang after a fashion and read aloud.

There is a hygiene of instruction for drawing as well as singing, for drawing, like other subjects, is a matter depending on nerves, muscles, and a brain. But this fact became clear only when children began to have great difficulty in doing very simple work, and even got ill as the result of such work.

That there is a hygiene of instruction in mathematics we know, because children have been injured physically by learning in the wrong way, and strengthened physically and morally by learning in the right one. Moreover, they "hated" the wrong movement, just as they would hate having their fingers twisted backward, but they enjoyed the right one, just as they enjoy walking and jumping.

Strangely enough, Britain, though tardy in going forward, has already sent out the school doctors who have more than others flung themselves into this higher order of work. They have begun to study the hygiene of instruction—a subject hardly mentioned by Continental doctors yet—and they are carrying it on with a good deal of ardour. And the teachers have not only helped them, but without the teachers' help it would have been impossible for the doctor to have attempted it.

It is common nowadays to map the brain off into three different levels, though there are, of course, no separate "levels" in fact. Still it is found convenient to speak of the " lower level," the " middle level," and the "higher level." In recent days even every one of these has suffered as the result of "schooling." The higher level is, as already stated, even to-day an unexplored country, more or less ; but a good deal can be learned about it through the study of the lower and middle regions.

The lower level includes, of course, all the spinal system, whose branches, flung wide and lying deep, have to do with the movements and life of the big organs—the heart, the lungs, the viscera. Strong and stubborn is the grip of life in these underground regions, and in infancy and early childhood the tides of life seem to toss and boil there just as water does in a cavern ere it has forced a way between the cliffs. But until the school doctor arrived this gathering together of energy was discouraged. It was drained off—that energy—in little wearing tasks This misfortune happened to a generation—but not to many generations, else one cannot tell what would have been the result. For education is openly, almost grossly physical, in its early stages. Young, vigorous races, and especially the great men of these, appear to be subject to great shocks and upheavals of every organ, and to be more conscious than are later generations of the intensity of the life fermenting in them. Thus, for example, the Psalmist in his outpourings speaks of his heart, of the viscera, of the bones even, continually, and, as it seems, of necessity. In less primitive people the response of the organism is much less violent and general ; and perhaps this is why teachers, for centuries and in every land, have been in such haste to make short cuts to the higher brain. But it is pretty well established now that this haste does not advance things—that to reach the higher levels too quickly is to arrive there with nothing of any value—with nothing to be worked up in the crucible of the higher centres. The great and deep channels of the sympathetic system—the system of nerves that run to all the great organs of the trunk—must have filled and must reverberate with all the swelling tides of life, in order to pour at last into new channels and feed the higher brain centres from their abundance.

So it was found that the formal school lesson is, for infants, not only a waste of time, but an unhygienic exercise—that it prevented the full exercise of regions that should be, early in the life history, in full functional activity. "How few young children are allowed to remain *with wandering mind* on the knees of their good mothers, touching, dreaming in peace . . . and coming forth from this baptism of emotion thinkers, discoverers, poets, saviours. . . ." Thus wrote Séguin many years ago.

The French word "égarer," which I have translated as "wandering mind," indicates here surely, not mind astray, but mind in the making.

To turn now to the middle brain. A little while ago it was an unknown land. But of late years a great many explorers have been busy with it, and a search-light has been thrown into some of its dark places. Thanks to them we have learned that this is *the* great storehouse of the brain—the place where things are kept for future use. It has many storage-places, and they are very elastic   They grow with the demand on their resources, and perfectly new chambers are built in when the demand for them exists. The eye, the ear, the nose, the skin, all have their own storerooms here, and what comes in through these senses is piled up in its own place as memories—reminiscences laid away, not on wooden shelves, however, but in rafts of living cells, and capable at any moment of being launched with great éclat into the vortex of the higher brain life. Here is the home of the subconscious mind. It can be readily seen why it is not well to examine too much, to interfere when a child is thoughtful or absorbed, or at play, or even idling.

In later ages, as we have seen, perfectly new memory chambers have been formed in the brain—centres for word-sounds, for example, and for written symbols. And some probably that were once wide are now shrinking a little, for it would seem that neglected brain-shelves tend to disappear. (Mrs. Boole says that the children of ancient Greece had an instinct for geometry, that they had accumulated a store of memories, unconsciously, that made Euclid an easy book comparatively for them, but that our children do not gather such memories of space and place always in the open, so they have less instinct for geometry, and are not prepared to learn it out of books.) Many people are not yet well furnished with brain chambers for various kinds of memory. For example, the place for word-memories must be still small in the labourer's brain. He does not need many words. Still he needs more now than formerly, and his brain is modified in consequence. Then his fingers were once too stiff to hold a pen, but now he can write, however stiffly or slowly. In short, many doors which were fast locked before are now being opened. There is probably no brain that is equally well developed in every part. In every one there are empty and shrunken chambers, and even gaps or rooms entirely missing, and sometimes a room may be crowded out altogether, as happens in the case of people who specialize too much or too early.

But, as we have seen, the middle brain is not a mere granary—or place where needful things are stored. It is a laboratory—the place in which at last what was mere vibration of air or ether is

changed into something new and strange.   Here are
united the tumultuous life from the lower centres,
and the mysterious life above.   The middle brain is
the outposts of the realm of intellect, of judgment,
of all the highest activities.   Within its depths the
impressions of every special sense are quickened,
condensed, worked up, and launched forward to the
higher centres.   Where this laboratory is richly
furnished, the mental life is apt to be rich also and
fertile.   Where it is scanty there is barrenness.   The
poor suffer much from hunger, from want of bread,
but also from lack of stimulus.   Monotony is starvation of the cerebrum.   Monotony of work is a kind
of privation.   The majority to-day have, as we have
seen, too small a range of work, of interest, and
emotion.   The winds of life do not reach the
strings of the human instrument freely enough,
and nature draws back the gift she was on the point
of offering.

The middle brain is the motor brain.   We could
have guessed as much from the restlessness of childhood.   But science has now put the matter beyond
dispute.   We might have guessed almost that here
is the capital of the higher and finer movements—
the movements that are willed, and learned.   For it
is a matter of common observation that there is a

time in life when one can learn languages easily,
and can manage to learn to play instruments well,
and when, moreover, we are very restless, and on the
look out for new kinds of movement ; a time when
a workshop is entered eagerly; and this period is
childhood and early boyhood or girlhood.   In elementary school children the middle brain is having
its spring-tide.   The spring-tide is short, and it does
not return.

And yet this middle brain—the great centre of
movement is also the Mecca of the indolent.   When
some kind of movement or activity has been perfectly learned the upper brain ceases to pay any
more attention to it, and is free for other tasks.   But
if the power of *attention* is not kept alive, and given
a new task, education proper ceases.   "The absence
of training of attention," says Dr. Kerr, "means
almost automatic reading, writing, or speaking of
a comparatively useless character educationally, as
it is done without effort and scarcely rises above the
threshold of consciousness."   In such exercises the
middle brain is working like a machine.   *A great
deal of the school work of the present day is of this
kind.*

The tendency of State education is to make the
middle brain its goal.

L

But what *is* that goal beyond—that higher level for which all the rest of the human system seems to labour and travail. What are those vast, silent areas, whose work is carried on in a darkness which has not been penetrated, and which seem to hold fast locked in their open yet silent hearts the mystery of our moral and mental life. Some things we know of them, that their action for example is largely one of restraint, of inhibition—that, in part at least, they act like the brakes on a machine, powerful brakes that can arrest the headlong course of primitive impulse.

Arresting power is here, and transforming power is also here, a new power of elaboration, and its exercise is seen in qualities that are more and more dominating the advancing race. And here too there is, almost certainly the same order of provision, the same kind of *mechanical* arrangements that determine progress of a less inspiring order. Just as there are word-storage places that make possible the development of speech and writing, so there is a storage of memories that makes possible the birth of a moral sense. Where are these memories, re lating to conduct and feeling, stored? "We cannot localize them," says one of the latest and ablest specialists on this subject. "They are a very late evolution. But we are pretty certain that for them also there *is* a receiving station—a storage place." In short, the whole body is laid under contribution, and the nervous system specially designed, for a life so great and wonderful that we have not even begun to appreciate it. And in every child born there is the desire to achieve that life. In every child that desire struggles on, glancing through all his impulses, interests, and affinities. It may be balked in myriads, it is balked in myriads. It is arrested, turned back ; but it persists while life lasts, so that even the diseased make haste to seize life, to enjoy and advance, and the defective are roused at times and press forward. Yes! the great army advances boldly, and what we begin to say in the modern school is briefly this : " They are to be suffered to advance. They are not to be turned back."

It is a great admission. For ages their path was made difficult. The scholasticism of the Middle Ages fell like a weight on the youth of the age. Its iron hand is not yet quite withdrawn. But now it is to be removed we hope, and what is more, the obstruction in the organism itself is to be searched out and removed if possible. The gates are to be lifted up, that the glory of life may enter. . . .

And the school doctor is here to hold us to that. He is to diagnose, not only disease, but faculty, and to discover the terrible secrets of success and failure where alone they are hidden—that is to say, in the organism.

CHAPTER X

THE SCHOOL DOCTOR IN OTHER LANDS

I T is clear that, in a sense, the school doctor has always existed. Wherever the inspired teacher was, there was he. For a long time, however, for more than a century, the voices of certain medical men have been crying in the wilderness that the condition of children should be observed and considered. There were such voices crying in England, and also in Germany; but little notice was taken of them in either country. At last in 1867 a German, Hermann Cohn, published notes on the vision of children, which went to show that the German nation was rapidly becoming short-sighted. Many doctors have since noted the sad effect of poverty and evil conditions on the eyesight. Cohn saw that the vision of children was threatened by one set of causes at home, and by others (such as bad lighting, small print, and so on) at school, and he put the result of all this before the public in such a way that he gained the ear of the authorities at last. He, with Erisman, shares the honour of being, perhaps, the greatest pioneer modern school doctor.

Nevertheless, Germany was slow to take action. She let other nations take the plunge before her. Thus, as Schubart, an eminent German school doctor, in his book *Schubartzwesen* points out, Brussels was the pioneer city in this work, for in 1874 she made provision for medical inspection in schools. Paris came next in 1879, Antwerp in 1882, Hungary in 1887, and Moscow in 1888.

The amount of inspection, and the nature of it, varied very much in these different places, yet they had all made a beginning of some kind before Germany or England took any practical steps at all.

Germany had a very good example of what real medical inspection can do to banish disease in her own army. During the first half of the nineteenth century 14 per thousand died in the Prussian army, and 10 per thousand of the civilians of like age. But in 1903 only 2·1 per thousand of the German army died, and among the civilians 5·2 per thousand.

"From the year 1873 to 1903," writes Hartmann, the chief school medical officer of Berlin, "the mortality of the people fell by two-thirds! In 1903 two and a half million 'sick list' days were saved, and seven hundred thousand of these would have been spent in hospital. That means a yearly saving of more than a million marks! And while the death rate was reduced by two-thirds, the amount of sickness was reduced by half. For instead of 67 per thousand of all the garrison being in hospital as formerly, there were now only three and a half. The hospital expenses too were lessened by one half. This happy result was attained only when an independent department for military sanitation—a department with a doctor at the head of it—was appointed. This, as the Report shows, gives quite obvious reasons why the development of sanitation in the army should be helped forward."

At the door of the school however the reformer hesitated long. The army results were good, but it was felt that to bring the doctor across the school threshold was a serious thing! To begin with, was it not an interference with parental rights? And then—the teacher! Was it not wrong to bring into the school a visitor who might interfere with *him* and make trouble? Ach Himmel! And finally, could not the teacher himself do all that was necessary instead of the school doctor? After all he, the teacher, perhaps knew something about Hygiene.

The first hesitations and objections are based

in every land, it seems, on almost the same grounds, but it is noticeable that the Germans, though frugal, never raised the bugbear of expense. They knew, from the first, that if school doctoring was worth anything it would be worth a great deal. They knew, as every one knows who watches the exchequer, that disease is very costly indeed. And they held back only in order to make sure of their ground! At last, in 1891, Leipzic took the plunge, and engaged the first German school doctor. In 1893 Dresden followed her example. As a matter of fact Germany was not then more forward than England, for in 1891 the London School Board engaged its first school doctor, and in 1893, at Bradford, Dr. Kerr entered on his half time duties as medical adviser of the School Board of that city.

Germany then was not at that time in the van. On the contrary, she was in the rear of many nations, and in line only with England. It would seem also that, in spite of the teachings of Cohn, and of other pioneers, she had not followed very closely the work of physicians and medical teachers (such as Séguin) in other lands, for the ideas in vogue in Germany as to what a school doctor's duties should be were still very vague. It was supposed that he should begin by inspecting school buildings. And a very alarming kind of duty this was too, to make his entrance with. For suppose he condemned many even of the new and expensive schools just built, and all by a stroke of the pen! A school doctor it was supposed should pronounce on questions of heating, lighting, ventilation, sanitation. So far his duties were something like a plumber's! Over and above this he would have something to do in preventing the spread of infectious disease! Such were the duties of a school doctor according to public opinion even in Germany in what is now called the "pre-Wiesbaden epoch" (Vor Wiesbadener Epoche).

Wiesbaden, famous as a watering place, famous once also as a gambling den, was destined to make for itself a new kind of renown. Situated on the slope of Mount Taunus, surrounded by fertile valleys, wooded hills, and villages bright with gardens and vineyards, furnished too with hot springs, Wiesbaden draws thousands of sufferers every summer to breathe its mild and yet bracing air. The town has been a kind of shrine of health always. Perhaps the sight of the invalids arriving in a constant stream urged the educational authorities to save their own townspeople from suffering by making every school a kind of health centre. Perhaps the people, who number many boarding-house keepers, wanted to show strangers what health is! In any case, the school doctor was never regarded by them as a mere inspector of buildings and detector of infectious disease. From the very beginning—that is to say, from the year 1896—he was given the task of discovering the bodily and mental condition of every child entering school. But what is more, this new knowledge was made the basis of the future training and teaching provided for the children. Thus Wiesbaden inaugurated a new epoch in elementary education. So tactfully and yet so boldly was the new work begun and carried on that within a year some of the large cities began to form their system of medical inspection on the plan furnished by Wiesbaden. But, what is more wonderful, Germany, which had been, up till the time that Wiesbaden took action, very doubtful and slow in developing any system at all of medical school inspection, now started forward like a man whose eyes have been suddenly opened, and made rapid progress. In a few years many hundreds of school doctors were engaged. They number now in all between six and seven hundred! And through the length and breadth of the Fatherland, Wiesbaden's methods have become more or less the classic of these doctors. Some have improved on them in certain

details, but Wiesbaden remains the centre of reference
and comparison for a great part of the work. Finally
this system was recommended in 1898 by the Prussian
Ministry. For these reasons we may take it as the
basis of all school medical inspections in Germany,
and must give some details of it.

. . . . . .

To begin with Wiesbaden not only respected the
rights of parents; it began by taking them entirely
into its confidence. A circular is sent out to every
parent in the first year of every child's school life.
It is really a long and confidential letter (very
unlike the leaflets issued from time to time by the
British educational authorities). It runs as follows:

" For the better protection of the health of children
attending the public schools, school doctors have
been engaged to undertake the medical inspection
of children on entering school, to be responsible for
their health as long as they attend the school, and
responsible too for the building itself from the point
of view of the scholars' health.

" These provisions will be of great use both to the
children and their parents. In the course of his
education, much will be learned with regard to the
health and bodily condition of each child, and this
new knowledge, which is being gained now for the
first time, the school doctors will put at the disposal

of the parents with whom henceforward they will work in the interests of the children.

"Parents who, however, do not wish that their children should be examined by school doctors have a right to exempt them, as the new provisions do not refer to educational matters that are in any way compulsory. Such parents however must furnish the necessary information from their own doctor."

They would be strange parents who would "take offence" on receiving such a letter as this. With this letter there is enclosed another, which requests, in case the examination is agreed to, the presence of the father, mother, or guardian.

Wiesbaden had not to create any precedent in so far as the details of this entrance examination is concerned. Already in 1887 Hungary had furnished her with a very good example. In the Hungarian Minute of twenty years ago it is set forth that "in the examination of new scholars, held at the beginning of every year, the doctor shall satisfy himself as to the health and condition of all children, more especially giving attention to the heart and lungs, and make known to the teachers whether children can take the usual physical exercises or drill, singing, etc. He will also test the eyesight, and the colour sense, examine ears, teeth, and report on any speech defect, also on any tendency to curvature. He will note the presence of any hair or skin disease," etc. Wiesbaden seems to have taken all this, but she added something of her own, for her formula of examination reads thus : "General constitution, height, weight, chest girth, chest and body organs, skin disease, spine and extremities, eyes and vision, ears and hearing power, mouth, nose, and speech, special remarks to teachers for the treatment in school, communications to the parents."

Such is the scope of the great entrance physical examination.[1] It leaves the school doctor, if he be worthy the name, aware of the child's state and prospects. This light is gained at the very threshold of the child's school life. It is won in the presence of the mother or guardian, and to give it to her is the first and great duty of the German school doctor. No one who reads the records can

[1] There is now in Wiesbaden and many other cities a preliminary inspection by the doctors to find out which children are ready for school life, and which had better remain at home for a while. A certain number of little ones are sent back to home-life for a while. Those who are allowed to begin school life are not examined for some weeks, so that they may get used to their surroundings. (Before the doctor's visit they rehearse, with the teachers, part of the proceedings, more especially if he is going to test ears and eyes—though, in many places, this testing of the higher sense-organs is done a little later in the school life.)

be in any doubt on this point. Nearly every German writer on the subject turns aside to emphasise the importance of it—to show that here is one of the greatest opportunities that can ever be enjoyed by any citizen. " The education authorities of many cities have the *desire* to reach the parents," says Schubart. " They find a great and new opportunity in meeting them. A school doctor who sees the real scope of his work appreciates this fact." It seems that nearly all are eager to speak to the parents at the examination. And the acquaintance does not end here for they send out circular letters asking for information. They send out letters, too, throughout the whole of the child's school life, giving information or warning. Strange it is to see how prophesy has *not* been fulfilled, how just the opposite thing has happened to what was prophesied. It was foretold that parental responsibility would be wiped out. It is noted that parental responsibility is created and developed on a large scale—the supply answering wonderfully to the new demand.

Thorough as the entrance examination is, it is not assumed to be anything more than a general diagnosis. It does not, in case of illness, take the place of a full home examination. The immediate aims of the school doctor are to give warning, to prevent injury (through school work and life), and to safeguard the sick and also the healthy. They are, I admit, restricted. They are other than those of the home doctor who treats "a case" in the home or hospital. But the examination is thorough so far as it goes, and can be undertaken only by an expert. This is proved merely by the fact that a large number of children who appear quite well, and awaken no anxiety at all, even in the breasts of the most careful parents, betray to the eye of the doctor the signs of coming illness, the unsuspected symptoms of future trouble.

The school examination is carried out rapidly—though, of course, cases vary much as to the time required. The healthy children pass merrily through it in a very few minutes. Dr. Speiss, of Frankfurt, writes : " The examination of a child entering school takes from 7 to 9 minutes. In many cases, however, it takes less time. (Dr. Arkell, of Liverpool, finds that three minutes will do, which seems a very short time.) However, it appears certain that even the examination of a diseased child does not take long. It is the examination that follows on treatment, not the first general examination, that requires time and patience.

After the first examination each child gets a health

card, which the teacher keeps.   There are three orders
of card—"Good," "Fair," and "Bad."   The first card is
that of the healthy children—the "good" group.   In
the second are the children in "fair" health.   In the
third or "bad" group are the children who suffer from
some disease, or who are very weakly.   These are all
under "medical control," as their health card shows,
and they are seen by the doctor at every class visit
—that is, once a fortnight.   Their growth and con
dition are always under his observation, and also
of course, under the teacher's, who knows more or
less now what she is to expect from these children.

On the teacher falls also one important duty—that
of recording at regular intervals the weight and
stature of healthy and unhealthy children.

From the first Wiesbaden took the whole question
of weighing and measuring very seriously.   Dr. Paul
Schubart declares in his book, *The School Doctor in
Germany*, from which most of these facts are quoted,
that weighing and measuring in school has for the
school-doctor the same value, as a means of finding
out the condition of children, as has the thermometer
for the doctor who stands by a patient's sick-bed.
"There is, however, one great difference between
the thermometer and the measuring and weighing
machine " says Schubart.   "One cannot reckon on

the absolute increase of either weight or of stature —but only on the increase of either in relation to the other in the course of the school life. The measuring and weighing must be accurate, and finally they must be done regularly, at equal intervals, so that a child who is weighed and measured in March and September one year, is not weighed and measured in April and October the next! If irregularly done the thing has no value, but well done, it gives indications so true and delicate that the weighing and measuring machines are looked on by some teachers as a kind of mental and moral barometer, rarely if ever at fault!

The Wiesbaden order on this point has been adopted by nearly all German towns. It runs as follows.—

"The weighing and measuring of children will be done by the class teachers. It is to be carried out half-yearly (measurement to half-centimetre and weight to one quarter of kilogramme). The doctor will measure regularly the chest girth of all children who are suspected of having lung disease, or whose constitution and health is such that they are under medical control."

The health sheet and the weighing and measuring machines bring home to teachers the fact that the

M

healthy children are passing rapidly through certain stages of growth, and that in the course of time the contrast presented by them to the under-nourished and undergrown gets more and more marked.[1] Never again will they have to attempt to make all toe the same line!

The Wiesbaden school doctors make a further examination of children in the third year of their school life—yet another in the fifth year. Finally, in the eighth and last year, just before the child leaves school, there is a final examination. The doctor has by this time his health card during school life before him. He has had opportunities of watching his progress, and has the teachers' report to help him. Thus he is more or less in a position to give advice to the parents which should be of use to them in choosing his future trade or career in life. And to do this is his parting service to pupil and parent.

But these great bi- and tri-ennial examinations are not the only occasions when the school doctor makes his rounds. Over and above them he has what are called his speech or consultation hours (Sprechstunde)

---

[1] This is very well illustrated in Dr. Arkell's figures. It is seen in the health sheets and records kept by school doctors in all lands—and is quite as noticeable, according to the reports, in Japan as in England.

at very short intervals. On these school visits he takes special note of all the children with "bad" health sheets. He looks into various parts of the building, and notes the lighting, warming and ventilation, and sanitation. It may be well to quote part of the Minute in the Wiesbaden scheme in which his duties are indicated.

"Every fourteen days the school doctor will hold a School Consultation at an hour fixed by doctor and head teacher. A certain room is to be placed at his service. . . . The first half of the hour will serve for a visit of from 10 to 15 minutes to be paid to from two to five Classes, during the time when the scholars are being taught.

Every class shall, if possible, be visited twice in every half-year. On these occasions all the children will be inspected, the teacher giving his observations and receiving the doctor's. If some of the children appear to be in need of special medical care, this fact is to be made known at these consultations.

On these visits the doctor can also take note of the sanitary conditions, the ventilation, heating. He will also note the bearing of the children. In making any remarks on the methods of the teacher, he will take care to avoid saying anything that can give offence. . . . The second half-hour will be spent in a more strict examination of certain cases. . . . The health sheet of every child will be inspected by the doctor.   The teacher will be present.

The giving of notices to the classes and assembling of the children will be done, of course, by teachers. (On the previous day the teacher will have observed what children should be examined, and will have sent out notices.)

If medical treatment appears to be necessary the parents are to receive information to that effect. They—the parents—are at liberty to choose what doctor they will employ, but the letter should contain a recommendation of any specialist treatment which may be required in any case.   Older children may take this kind of information home and report it by word of mouth ; but in the case of younger children, or where the word of mouth report has not been attended to, a printed letter (for which there is a form), should be filled in and sent. This is to be done, of course, only in cases of real illness and where the interest of the child and of the school demands it.   In the filling in of these forms great care is to be taken not to give offence through hardness or roughness of expression."

The earnest effort of the Wiesbaden authorities to get in touch with parents, to enlighten without estranging them, has certainly met with wonderful success.   About forty towns have adopted the Wies baden scheme *in toto*. A great many other towns and districts have, as we have said already, adopted the general scheme, but altered the details. In some of these the consultation (or speech hour) is held only once in three months or once in six months. Doctors everywhere appear to be in touch with parents, to send full reports to them, and to invite their co-operation. Take, for example, a quotation from the letter sent by the Giessen school authorities to the parents of children in whom the first signs of spinal curvature have been noted by the school doctor: "The school teachers will take full notice of these symptoms in the school work for the future; we, however, entreat you to consult your own doctor and to help us, so that a permanent curvature may be averted."

Whether it be the result of the tact and gentleness of the method or whether due to some spontaneous awakening, it is hard to say. But certain it is that all over the Fatherland parents have responded and placed themselves on the side of the school doctor. The response comes, not only from the big towns; it is most hearty and practical in some of the little out-of-the-way villages.[1]

[1] It seems that in one of these—Kallstadt—a village of from 1100 to 1200 inhabitants and with from 150 to 160 school children, a school

In fact, the desire for this new Eye in the school
seems to have asserted itself and freed itself from
the spirit of mere officialism, so that the movement
develops here and there in most unexpected ways,
and even shows in some places great freedom and
originality.   It is a people's movement, born in a
state-governed country.   In ten years one-fifth of
all the German people have caused their children
to be educated under the eyes of a school doctor.
The whole movement seems to have united a great
boldness with great confidence on the part of the
people and of the school authorities.   As evidence of
the confidence, there is the fact that, though examination by the school doctor is not compulsory,
barely 4 per cent of all the parents have preferred to
have their children examined at home, and even this
percentage was reached only because 9·5 per cent
of the middle-class (Burgherschule) withdrew their
children.   Only 1·1 per cent of the working people
have withdrawn *their* children.   And the information
they receive is not flung away.   Leipzic reports that
three-fourths of all the parents of delicate and

doctor is engaged to visit the school every three months, and to note
those who are ill and give information to the parents.   For these
services he receives twenty-five marks a year, and for every child
examined a fee of four pfennige !

diseased children act at once on the advice offered. Only 3·5 per cent neglect a second warning. In some cities—in Mulhausen and Berlin at least— they (the parents) are invited to the conferences of teachers and doctors. Schubart sums up the position by saying: "Of any serious objection on the part of parents to the school doctor nothing is heard."

What is the result of medical inspection? We may perhaps ask the question of Wiesbaden, since Wiesbaden has attempted to do the work so thoroughly. She has a population of only 86,000. Yet Wiesbaden has seven school doctors for her nine or ten thousand children, whereas London has twenty or twenty-one doctors, but nearly all of them are not even half-timers, but give only *a quarter* of their time to the half a million of children in her schools. The countries who have hesitated long will want, then, to ask the question: What is *the result* of all your courage and labour? The answer seems, briefly, to be as follows:—

In a matter of this kind results on paper, if fully and accurately worked, would have a great value. But no one can pretend that these can be had in a moment. To begin with, there is no standard of comparison between children to-day who have gone through the eight years of school life and children of the same age in 1896, when school doctor's work was fairly started. And then it is well known that through the eight years of elementary school life—say from six to fourteen—children do grow out of certain weaknesses, and the life risks are getting less. Infancy's miseries wither in this impulse; they are sloughed off like a withered sheath, in the children who escape. So the following table, though it is interesting and clearly indicates that school life has strengthened rather than (as in old days) injured the scholars, does not, of course, offer the full and complete evidence which will be, we believe, soon forthcoming. (The classes are numbered, it seems, in the reverse order of ours. Thus our ex-seventh and highest standard is called the first here, and the lowest—our first standard—is called the eighth.)

HEALTH AND CONSTITUTION OF CHILDREN OF SECONDARY SCHOOLS (MITTELSCHULEN).

Classes.	VIII.	VI.	IV.	I.
Good .	. 39·6 ...	47·8 ...	64·0 ...	65·3
Fair .	. 59·2 ...	51·6 ...	35·3 ...	34·7
Bad .	. 1·2 ...	0·6 ...	0·7 ...	—

So much for the well-to-do children, who would seem from this table to get the better of disease entirely by the time they are nine or ten, though, as a matter of fact, this is not exactly what happens. What happens is that the sickly or defective do not go forward. Still, the table is cheering as showing how vigorous, on the whole, and how bold, is the upward swing of life.

The same upward movement is found in the elementary school, though it is not, unhappily, so striking there.

CONSTITUTION OF CHILDREN IN ELEMENTARY
SCHOOLS (VOLKSCHULEN)

Classes.	VIII.	VI.	IV.	I.
Good .	. 27·8 ...	37·6 ...	35·6 ...	48·1
Fair .	. 67·4 ...	57·4 ...	62·5 ...	50·6
Bad .	. 4·8 ...	5·0 ...	1·9 ...	1·3

What part school doctoring has played in helping this upward movement we cannot yet learn — absolutely. There are other means of marking it, however, than the gathering of statistics, important as these are. Happily there is no need to wait long, no need to be an expert, in order to make every-day observations. These *are* made, and they are after all so reliable, generally speaking, that we all live and move, and are here to improve our methods of registering changes simply because, from our birth, and long before it, people were making observations and getting "results" that were trustworthy and acting on these. "Science" is only an extension or refinement of common sense and common observation, and to know the effect of the school doctor's work in Germany, we may take this kind of witness as well as the other. It appears, then, that medical inspection has had the effect of lightening, in many respects, the work of the teachers. On the whole it has lightened it so much that, even when all the new work is reckoned, it has brought, not a strain, but relief. The compulsion to attempt to make all children, sick or well, ill or well endowed, normal or abnormal, toe the line and reach one standard is given up. Moreover, if a child fails to-day, it is no longer at once surmised that the teacher is at fault. All this constitutes such a relief from the thrall of blind Power that the mere weighing, measuring and observing of children is a small burden in comparison.

To come now to more definite instances of successes attained through new departures for which the doctor is responsible.

At Mannheim there are "Hilfsklasse," or classes

for backward children. We have already seen how from 10 to 20 per cent of all children go to these for a shorter or longer time; and how, at Mannheim, many are more than ready after a time to go back to the ordinary school. This kind of "result" is being welcomed all the time by doctor, teacher, and parent, and it is altogether the result of training that is largely treatment. For in such schools the doctor is in a sense the head master, inasmuch as he is responsible for the order of the teaching, and all the details of the work, in a very special way.

Then the school bathing has had results. It has even results on paper. For it is found that only 1·8 per cent of all the children have to be classed as not clean. (Contrast this with our figures in Britain —the dreadful fact that one English doctor estimates that only 30 per cent of our children are clean and that nearly 35 per cent are in a horrible state; that another writes that in some districts 45 per cent are very dirty, and only 12 per cent clean ; and that yet another declares that taking an average roughly including children from various districts, 1 in 5 is very dirty.) Thus the class rooms have almost suddenly become safe and healthy places in comparison to what they once were, and in every city where the baths are installed there is a crowd of witnesses to tell how the children have grown brighter and fitter for work since this new subject was added to the curriculum.

Good results too seem to have followed the opening of special classes, especially of those for children who stammer. These receive speech and other physical training and many quickly get over their difficulties.

A word too, must be added, on the subject of the out-of-door school. It would appear that this really is in some respects the most promising departure of all! It is such, not merely because a large number of all the children who enter this kind of school recover health and strength. This is one "result"— but there are others, which are in the nature of a revelation! It seems that all the subjects have a new meaning for the children when they are taken out-of-doors. Arithmetic and geometry are no longer a kind of torture when they are studied as they were studied by the first mathematicians and reckoners, and when the foot, the hand, the arm, are again used as means of measurement. The first problems are solved on the grass or in the sand. The writing lesson becomes simple and easy. Writing is a tempting occupation outside, as one can see by looking at rocks and out-door seats. The little ones draw out-of-doors with a will, as the Bushmen drew, and as the great Eastern artists still sometimes draw. Even the first " R " is learned rapidly outside. (In many a church and chapel magazine, missionaries tell how quickly the Red Indians and others learn reading in the open.) Out in the open, doubtless, every little hand would eagerly project itself. There everything invites, impels even, to self-projection. There tools are made eagerly. There the whole value of play declares itself, and exercise does not consist in formal walking or mere aimless running! In short, out of doors the healthy child finds (in good weather, at least) the ideal school! It is not easy to see how it can quickly be restored to all, or even to many. Who knows how many years may pass before we can even give a roof playground to all the pale-faced children of the cities? For a long time, as it appears, we must be content, in our climate, to build schools for rude weather, to think of fog, and frost, and rain, and trust a very great deal to the power of pictures, of good ventilation, and of symbols.

Already however the sickly children gathered out of the school population of Charlottenburg and Mulhausen are at their beneficent work. They are showing, as the feeble have always shown, where the new light falls. They are drawing us back, as is their wont into the far, far past—and are pointing also with their pale fingers, into the far future.

Only weakness can be so bold and so convincing.

.   .   .   .   .   .

It is strange but true, that thoughts seem to pass like a wind from one civilized country to another, or rather to encircle them all in one mysterious and rapid movement. The recent sudden awakening as to the needs of child life in every country is a case in point. The first school doctors were formally engaged in England and in Germany in the same year, 1891. The first American school doctor was formally appointed at Boston in 1894. In 1896 the first steps were taken at Wiesbaden to put medical inspection of schools in Germany on a firm basis. In 1897 the first Cleansing Committee was formed in England. In 1896 the first Board of advice for School Hygiene was instituted by an Imperial Ordnance in Japan. In the same year the New World of the West roused herself suddenly like a young eagle. For seven years New York had been putting her huge house in order as regards school children's health and conditions with such fiery haste and zeal that everything one writes on the subject seems to be old before the ink is dry. She is hurrying past all the time. " In a few years," her senior school doctor cries to us gaily, " we shall, so far at least as physical conditions are concerned, have no lower classes."

That is a very cheering thing to hear. And the best of it is that it appears to be *true.* America is the country where huge fortunes are quickly make, and quickly lost. Its citizens have something of the ardour of the South, and also something of the sense of impermanency in all things, that distinguishes the far East. So they make haste to grow rich, and being rich do not as a rule hug their gold tightly. Rich men are found in numbers who will endow costly institutions and schools, and pay for new public experiments. So money was no bar, once the idea had occurred to the city fathers to make the young citizens clean and healthy. In 1897 New York actually engaged a hundred and fifty doctors, each of whom would have the care of only three to five schools. A corps of nurses was also engaged and a health squad formed in the police force to go round and visit homes where there were infectious cases. Such measures as these do not re-create a race, or make everyone healthy. But they certainly are designed to give a rude set-back to infectious diseases and to lift the incubus that results from

neglect, off the lives of myriads.   They lift it as
suddenly as one raises a stone and sets the creatures
below into a panic: and this, apparently, is what
happened in New York.   The Report of Dr. Thomas
Darlington, Commissioner of Health for 1905 (a copy
of which is kindly lent to me by Mr. T. Sykes),
shows that whereas in 1903 there were 32,525 children excluded for eye diseases, the number fell in
1905 to 8883—that the number of cases of contagious skin diseases fell from 4000 to 2018; and that
whereas 21,100 were in a sadly neglected state in
1905 only 4692 were still doomed to live as human
beings should not live.   In short, the number of
excluded children fell from 65,294 to 18,844; though
the school population must have increased.   All this
seems to bear out the claim of the senior school
doctor.

However, we need not dwell here on the American
system—bold as it is.   Let us turn from the West,
with its courage and its gold, to the Far East, with its
modest standard of life, and its soaring ideal! Japan
has been in the whirlwind of reform.   She begins
however by an open confession.   "We want school
doctors," says the Education Report from Japan of
1903–4, "but we have not got enough trained men.
We cannot make provision yet for all."   Still, she

has made a beginning. In 1899 the number of school doctors in Japan was 2906. But in 1903–4 the number had risen to 4941. The allowances for school doctors seem very small. The salary of the permanent medical adviser of the Government Board of Hygiene is 500 yen, or about £100. The Government grant in 1899 was only 27·20 yen per head, and in 1903 this was raised to 29·13 yen. That is to say, the government makes a grant for medical school inspection of over £32,000 per annum.

This is a small sum, and the payment made by local bodies is doubtless on the same scale. And what does medical inspection of schools in Japan consist of? It would seem that the doctors undertake many of the duties that are performed by European school doctors. They examine eyes and test vision. They measure and weigh pupils and advise as to the treatment of the diseased and defective, and they send reports to the minister of state for education who, in his turn places them before a board appointed to consider matters of school hygiene. On this board of nine members there are three doctors—that is to say there is a medical staff at headquarters. So it appears that Japan, in spite of her gentle disclaimers, is ahead of us in some respects.

N

Yet their task must be other than is that of the Western doctors! To begin with, *they* have not to face dreadful conditions of body, and uncleanness. It seems that in Japan even the poorest are clean, and the care of the skin and of the hair is not only brought to perfection, but it is quite general. It is an instinct of the entire race. The little dainty houses, too, that look like toys, are clean, and only the rich attempt to bar out the light and air a little. Everything is renewed continually, and Nature's changes and upheavals are always in evidence. Terrible spring cleanings are Nature's in Japan. There is a regular course arranged in every town for the study of earthquakes and volcanic eruptions, and the scholars learn how to build a little house that will rock safely without falling.[1] Hygiene is already so far advanced in some ways that one might feel the people had little to learn. Yet in spite of all there is a shadow side. The diet, the feeding of infants, seem to leave a great deal to be desired. It is hinted that the Japanese physique is a thwarted product— like their miniature trees!

In a Report published in 1904, the doctors' report

[1] All this is very practical. For, as many writers have shown, the face of the land and the shapes of the mountains change as the result of earthquakes and eruptions. Now and then there is a tremendous upheaval. One of these destroyed 14,000 little houses.

of a very large number of Japanese school children examined, runs :—

  42·1 per cent of good constitution
  50·8 per cent of fair or medium constitution
  7·1 per cent of weak constitution.

In a later Report, published in 1906, the figures are :—

  53·5 per cent strong
  43·3 per cent medium
  3·0 per cent weak.

Another Report, in which the two sexes are not grouped, gives the following result :—

	Healthy Constitution	Medium	Weak
Males . . .	49·2 ...	47·2 ...	3·80
Females . .	29·3 ...	49·9 ...	20·8

Of eye diseases we hear nothing at all ; but short-sightedness is common there as here, more especially among boys and men. The figures given in the last Report are :—

Normal sight	Short sight
63	36
86	14

The Reports are scanty, and give no details. They seem to show that improvement in physique may be rapid ; that the people may respond quickly to the new impulse to evolve new muscular power, since muscular power is wanted. Every one who visits Japan notes this great flexibility, a quickness and delicacy of response to the call of the hour. It reminds one of their own paper windows that reflect every shadow. Responsive and flexible, they sway now towards a new order of physical development, and that they are capable of this is shown by the great differences of stature found among even the children. And the impulse that has come is strong—as witness the rapid increase in the number of physicians, the demand for more trained doctors, the teaching of hygiene to girls, etc.

Thus East and West are rising at last to fight disease, and to deal with defects of every kind. It is impossible that the opening years of this new campaign should be cheerful. The facts that come to light seem to be most depressing just in those lands where the battle is keenest and most determined. Thus in Germany, though some causes of disease have been removed of late, yet the consciousness of the real scope of the evil is growing. It seems greater now than it did ten or even five years ago. The workers stand like people going through a home that has been ravaged by fire. They note again and again how things that were forgotten, or believed to be safe, have really been lost or damaged. But this survey is not the herald of evil to come. It takes account of a past tragedy. To-morrow the house shall be re-built—on a safer and wider foundation. This is certainly not a day of rejoicing. But it is a day of hope.

CHAPTER XI

THE SCHOOL DOCTOR AT HOME

THE British school doctor exists, but so small is the number of men appointed to this post (they hardly number as yet fifty), and so greatly do the amount and nature of their work vary, that at present the phrase "school doctor" has no very clear meaning to many. Moreover, a great many people think that even if school children are examined, there need be no school doctor—that a medical officer of health will do quite well for this kind of work. It is clear that the British school doctor is hardly even a new arrival. He is a person who is being quarrelled over on the doorstep!

Not but that he has been allowed to look in and even to make a hurried round. In London the school doctor enters a school, looks, listens, examines some children, even weighs and measures a few; but *he* does not return as the Wiesbaden doctor returns, in a fortnight. He fares forth over a great wilderness, disappears like a cloud, and is perhaps seen only after a year has passed, and when many ailing children have gone forth to enter on their life struggle in bad health. Occasionally to be sure a man may make a study of one group of schools or of a single neighbourhood ; but the City is vast, the time of nearly all the school doctors is but a fragment (they are not all, as we saw, whole-timers—most of them are men in ordinary practice, giving a part of their time to this work), and all the schools have to receive a visit. No zeal or ability could make such work bear great practical results in so far as the children seen are concerned.

In provincial cities the position is a little different. Take Bradford for example. There the school doctor has to take a general oversight of forty thousand children ! By dint of labour he can see every class in every school more than once a year. One cannot deny that something may be done by such medical inspection of forty thousand children. But can any one pretend that all these children are safeguarded ? that all receive treatment ? or that the condition of of each can be learned and taken account of ?

Nevertheless, good work has been done in England. One may go further and say that work has been done here of a kind that is not yet even attempted in Germany. In reading the accounts of the German system we cannot but feel that the views on school doctor's work, though very definite, are wonderfully restricted. At first, and for a long time, as we saw, it was believed in Germany that this work had to do merely with school buildings. Then it was recognized that it should include the child—in so far as his state of health is concerned. Only to-day is a voice here and there heard crying that, beyond all this, the teaching itself and the training itself given in school has a physiological side ; that elementary education at least, is always more or less of a physiological experiment, and that for this reason, in elementary schools, the teachers and doctor should come a little closer together. Why should either confine himself to looking for disease ? Has the school doctor *no* interest in seeing and hearing a lesson given ? For a long time the German teachers seem to have looked askance at the school doctor, more particularly if he seemed to interrupt or disturb a lesson. He was careful not to "interrupt." He turned his eyes away from all teaching at first. But this feeling of utter separation between the teacher's and doctor's work is breaking down a little. He is now required to sit through lessons.

In England, I think it never existed—or hardly ever existed—this feeling of estrangement. One of

the first school doctors ever appointed in England
seems to have begun at the point which the Germans
are approaching, for he looked keenly at all the
school work ; he studied it from the distinctively
physiological point of view, and others followed his
example.   There were various reasons why they
should thus fly as if on wings to this kind of work.
As a matter of fact, they could hardly attempt
much of the preliminary work, important as it is !
They might, of course, and *did*, look at buildings.
They were keener on the subject of ventilation than
the German.[1]   But from across the Channel came
the axiom, "The school doctor must not attempt
treatment in any case.   That is not his work.   He
must simply inspect, notify, and give information."
That axiom came from little towns for the most part
— towns where the school doctor could have an
intimate conversation with nearly every parent, and
where he could keep up, by circular letters at
least, a regular correspondence with many towns
where teacher, doctor, and parent knew one another,
and were kept in touch by frequent meetings !   It
was fairly easy in such places to see that every child
had treatment who needed it !

[1] Not, of course, that we can pretend that all our schools, or even
the majority of them, are well ventilated.

But English city life is another story.   In the great industrial centres the school doctor's advice was very often flung away.   We know now that more than half of all the children are in such a condition that advice should be given about them to their parents!   But in the poorer schools only 3 per cent of the children needing spectacles get them. Of the 30 per cent of all the children who have adenoids, of the 8 per cent even who have this distressing ailment in a very acute form, the school doctor may have inspected a great number ; but how many even of these have received treatment?   And of these, how many are cured?   It is well known that these cases are often tedious, and parents cannot spare the time to go often to hospital.   A large number cannot, or do not even go once after being warned.   "He will grow out of it," they say of the sufferer.   So the case is neglected, and the patient becomes in many cases deaf for life.   Well, the school doctor cannot at present do anything—it is his business to note the evil, and then to leave everything to take its course—and hurry on to the next school.

For sixteen years the few men engaged in this work have known the limits of their powers so well that, almost unconsciously perhaps, they began to think of other matters than treatment.   They looked,

as we say, at school buildings like their German confrères.   But the thoughts of some happily took a
much wider range.   The hygiene of instruction is
more advanced here than in Germany.

Beginning in the infant school, they studied the
little ones.   They watched them drilling, drawing,
and learning their letters.   They brought their knowledge of a child brain and nervous system into the
infant room, and by-and-by new light was thrown
on old "occupations."   Things that Froebel did not
know were made clear to the infant-school mistress.
She began to see what a baby eye, a baby brain, and
baby muscles are.   But all the while she was not
simply a learner; she also had something to teach
the doctor, new as he was to one half of his whole
task.

Into the class rooms of older children too he, the
school doctor, passed, listened to the singing, looked
at the singers, and began to speak of things which
are not mentioned in song books, and to speak of
matters that are not dwelt on by many singing
masters, even among those who have degrees for
music and get splendid reports.   And he threw new
light on the teaching of drawing,[1] of languages, of

---

[1] It was the school doctor who showed, for example, the *real* meaning of bi-manual drawing, who showed how as crawling, on all fours,

the three R's. He noted nerve symptoms and spoke of these, gave lectures to the teachers of defective children (which were eagerly attended by some who were teaching the normal children), and made maps of the human brain in the presence of astonished and awakened teachers. The question of fatigue began under him to assume a new interest, and its signs were perceived at last and understood; and the meaning of child character and behaviour, the processes and order of growth, the order of development of human faculty — all began to become clearer, like the outline of things taking shape in the rising light of dawn. But still, in all this, the teacher was no passive recipient. He was giving and teaching—all the time. Perhaps it will never be really known what part each played in the new conquest of knowledge. The school was a strange place at first to the doctor. His knowledge of child-life was at first, I think, somewhat small. And the teacher's experience and training had a value that was perhaps never realized till it was

---

precedes walking on two feet the infant nervous system finds in the large inclusive movement the path to a finer one. It was he who showed why skeleton lines are an evasion of eye training, and who threw light on the various methods of teaching reading and spelling. It was he who interpreted symptoms and movements, who "explained" the sensory child and his reserve—and so on *ad infinitum.*

brought into touch with this new order of observer. However that may be, the progress made in a few years was extraordinary. It revolutionized in many ways the whole idea and method of teaching—in the small areas where doctor and teacher were working together. And the influence spread far beyond. It did not always reach the people in the next village. But it reached sometimes people who were far away! It reached Germany. All this could not have happened at first in Germany—where the teachers held aloof from the new "official." But it happened in England and indeed very little else was allowed, during these early years, to happen.

.   .   .   .   .   .

So now in either land we see the result of the past work. In Germany, where the people have done everything, and the State (with the exception of Hesse and Meiningen) nothing, there is a popular movement to bring the whole child population under the care of the school doctor, and to use the State and its power to insure the gains that have been won. All this is due, of course, to the way in which the work was approached. When the sick were made whole, and the stammering were made to speak, the parents saw very well the uses of the school doctor. And now, assured of their position, some of these doctors are looking further ahead and turning their thoughts to education itself as a physiological process. They were bound, of course, to come to this. No one, who deals with living things, can be thinking always of disease. The wild flowers are healthy enough. They fade quickly. The cultivated flower, the cultivated brain, has greater resources. It has its secrets to-day, its secret risks, its secret evils, its secret store of wealth. It is *very* interesting. Even the school doctor of Germany, moving about in schools every day, must have become conscious of all this. He too has become conscious of great events taking place as a result of the teaching given in the schools. The lesson, at which at first he was an intruder, must have begun, sooner or later, to have some interest for him. He was preparing all the while to see things that were dark to Froebel. He divined, too, that in upper schools there were secrets of life into whose heart he might glance as the varied appeal and labour of school life awakened new powers of response. And now he is at the gate of the fields into which his English confrères have broken like children who, not being allowed to go into the garden, have consoled themselves by getting into the orchard.

Meantime, though the work of gathering statistics goes on in our country, our schools are not centres of healing. " Examination " has a dismal sound in the ears of many. It seems to indicate a test, not an open door to health and new life. And very slowly though public opinion is changing, the great public come to see that they want this new kind of doctor. But it is said, if he *must* come, then why should we not engage the services of the medical men we employ already? We are a conservative people— why not engage a medical officer, or his assistant? That is briefly what many think.

There is, of course, the ever-present question of expense. It would cost a great deal of money to engage a vast army of medical men for these new posts. That, it is allowed, might spell economy if it stemmed the great flood of disease bearing social wreckage for ever into our hospitals. But of course it would mean a great initial expense. For you cannot get first-rate advice on a large scale without paying accordingly. First-rate advice, the service of highly trained and accomplished school doctors, is bound to be costly. This is what John Bull thinks, and his thoughts appear to be reasonable.

They *are* reasonable—only they do not take account of all the facts. The only persons who could answer John Bull in an altogether illuminating way are the ablest of our own school doctors. And it is unlikely, for various reasons, that they will undertake this task. This is why the mere looker-on has to attempt it.

It is of course necessary to have trained medical men to undertake the work of giving advice in (and treatment later probably through) the schools. This is so clear that it hardly needs to be emphasized at all. No trained nurse, no devoted mother, no clever teacher, no person in authority, can take the place of, or do the specific work of, a trained medical man or woman. And this special training is of course expensive, and those who receive it and give their services afterwards have, of course, a right to be paid at a reasonable rate.

But what does the phrase " a fully qualified school doctor" mean? Where are these "fully qualified" men to be found? The ablest and oldest school doctors know very well that they are not qualified—that they are only apprentices.[1] They also know

---

[1] An apprentice may, of course, be a great worker, a pioneer. The point is, not that his work is either great or small—the point is that at first it does not command money. He creates, among other things, its money value. Köhn examined the eyes of 10,000 children. His work is so valuable that no one can fully estimate it. But he got no money for it. He never got any. Dr. Kerr's work at Bradford was very valuable. His salary was extremely small.

that they have to make the school perhaps where
their successors will learn. For *them* there is no
college. A little while ago, when they began work,
they certainly did not even know that the new learning—the kingdom of knowledge that is now widening
out before their gaze—existed. They began, as we
saw, by looking at the buildings. They then began
to look at a great many children, and they saw that
more than half of these children were not quite well,
and that a great army of them were ill, and likely to
be soon very much worse. And only last of all did
they begin to see that learning, like eating, brings
certain parts of the body into activity, and that one
may learn something about the organ of thought as
well as about the organs of digestion. Yet as years
went by and new helpers were found in the school,
the new learning began to be gained. It is won, as
other kinds of knowledge are won, with effort and in
doubt, and often only after many fruitless attempts
and much labour. And now, though much has been
fairly earned, it is still the day of small things—all
the more because, after all, very few great scientists
will go into an elementary school class room and
think they have much to do with, or much to learn
from, child or teachers.

But when the school doctor hears that any kind of
    o

medical man—a medical officer, for example—will do for this work, he naturally feels that while he, himself, is a beginner, the majority of doctors have not even begun fairly to consider the needs of the schools. He feels that though there is no college for school doctors,[1] no chair, no Minister of Public Education, even, yet there *is* a new science of education. This is his discovery; or rather it is the discovery of the many doctors who have taken part for forty years or more in the study of the brain and the study of school children.

If the expert medical officer begins this work, he certainly cannot begin it as an expert. He may learn rapidly, but still he is a beginner. This will mean that he makes a sacrifice.

One does not begin, as one of the youngest apprentices, by receiving a large salary.

   .   .   .   .   .

[1] The medical faculty in Hungary have a special college for school doctors. Special courses and lectures for young school doctors are given in various cities, but such methods would be scouted for any other order of thorough professional training. One cannot learn this new work through attending lectures. Not but that some of the courses do of course afford a means of real training in certain departments of the work, as, for example, the class on the eyesight of school-children held lately by Köhn at Breslau. But as a matter of fact work in the schools, and the experience gained thus by doctors who have taken the ordinary diplomas, and whose attention is turned to scholastic problems, is the only means of getting an all-round training in England to-day. It is perhaps the best method. It certainly is the only one, and it gets rid of the question of fees.

The popular way of looking for the good school doctor is to offer him a large salary. And yet it does not work out very well. "If there is one thing I hate," said a certain medico the other day, "it is this school hygiene, and all this child-study that people are going in for now. It's all nonsense. All the same, *it is a good opening*. If they offer a decent salary, say £500 a year, I don't see why one shouldn't go in for it." And, indeed, there is no doubt that if a large number of very good salaries were offered to-morrow, a large number of fully qualified medical practitioners would apply ; but it is not at all so certain that these, if engaged, would advance the cause of education. It is much more likely that they would, for some time to come, set it back—perhaps set it back indefinitely. Obviously, this is not the way to find the right men. Where are they ? And is there a supply of living enthusiasts always on hand?

Strange to say, *there is*. And it is opportunity, not a bait, that is wanted to bring them into the field. Opportunity would be found for all, if, all over the land, education committees engaged medical men and women to take up it might be only a very small part of the whole duties of a school doctor. They might be engaged for example to visit a school twice or three times a year, and to report on the new scholars or on the sickly or abnormal children. They might, or might not, according to the desire of parents, be permitted to give treatment. They might take steps to prevent the spread of infection, and there is no child ailment which they might not, if they willed, specialize on, in so far as observation is concerned. The door would thus be opened to many, and that, at first, is all that is wanted. Many would enter, and every one would reveal himself, more or less. Their work might cost as much or as little as the parents willed. It might cost the merest trifle, as in many German villages. It should be open to them, as rate-payers, to extend it or to restrict it. But since parents are obliged to send their children to school, and since they have to take risks in doing so, the schools should be made, in so far as is possible, safe places. Therefore it is right that some degree of medical inspection of *all* elementary schools should be compulsory.

If once this was admitted, and if all schools had some kind and degree of medical inspection, then from every part of the country Medical Reports of some kind or another would begin to pour in at the head office of the Board of Education. Perhaps some of these Reports would come from men who, from the first, aspired to be genuine inspectors of

educational method, and not mere statisticians or
recorders of disease.   Almost certainly a fair number
would be genuine enthusiasts, attracted, not by the
pay (since the payment at first could not be a very
tempting bait), but by real love of the work.   Their
reports would then need consideration—the consideration of trained medicos, not of brilliant litterateurs,
or of politicians, or men of every and any order of
experience and education except that kind of knowledge that would make them able to judge of the
value of this new information.   And so we should
have to follow the example of Japan — and the
example of Germany.   A central medical board
would be wanted, not to frame cast-iron rules, or to
interfere with the new growth, but to *preserve* it and
keep for it a place where it may grow, if the living
impulse in it is strong enough.

Later there might be prizes, even many prizes, to
offer in this profession, as in others.   But they would
be won by service and self-devotion, not by influence
or through the ignorance of the public and at its
expense.   There are many victories—every man in
an army is a victor—towards the end of a battle, but
not at the beginning.   Workhouses, prisons, refuges—
great sums are spent in providing all these, and in
making deep channels as it were for the dark, swift

river of human misery that is flowing ever into the night of forgetfulness. Yet, need this river be so deep—so wide ? " No," say the school doctors standing at its source. " No," thunders even the merest tyro, perceiving how slight, how curable in the earlier stages are the fierce maladies that mow down at last the sons and daughters of poverty.

The day will come doubtless when the task of those who prevent illness will be thought more highly of   The day is nigh, perhaps, when the elementary school will have quite openly as its first great aim the conquest of health and sanity for its children.

.   .   .   .   .   .

Into the hands of the working people the guidance and control of education is bound to fall in an ever-growing degree as the years pass. They will be drawn into this work through their own children attending school, and sharing the life of the school. And they will be drawn into it also because they are bound to play a more and more important part in the counsel of the nation, and to become more conscious of the causes of its successes and its failures.

This growing power of the people is a thing in which every class of worker must rejoice at last and find his safety. For it cannot be well for a nation to fall under the power of any one class or profession,

be it the priest, the doctor, the teacher, or any other
It cannot be in the interest of science or progress
that any one of these should usurp power, for then
the mere love of this power, and the tyrannical use
of it, would take the place (as has been seen before)
of the higher hunger after knowledge, and the desire
for the conquest of disease.   So the old phrase,
"We must educate our master," may be amended so
as to run, "We must all, for our own safety and
freedom, allow the people to educate themselves in
the only new way in which they can be educated—
that is, by accepting responsibility."[1]

"But are they, the people, fit for it?" some voice
may cry; and the thought may occur to thousands of
plain and humble folks, "Are we indeed fit for it? Do
we know anything at all of education?" This book
serves no purpose at all, if it does not serve to show
that work, the rough labour of tillers of the ground,

[1] "For some years before the invention of electric telegraphy,"
writes Sir James Paget, M.D., "Professor Cummings of Cambridge,
when describing to his class the then recent discovery by Dersted of
the power of an electric current to deflect a magnet used to say,
'Here are the elements which would excellently serve for a system of
telegraphy.' Our successors will wonder at us," says Sir James
Paget, but perhaps they will not wonder, perhaps they will understand
why the brain loses power, and becomes active only in a very limited
degree when the stimulus of real work is withdrawn. It is possible
that all this lack of readiness and resource will be clear to them as
noonday, and that some kinds of cleverness will go out of fashion.

builders, sailors, carpenters, weavers, miners, foresters, iron-smelters, engineers, IS education. A strange sleep, an *absence of mind*, comes to even the brightest looking people who have never at any period of their lives engaged in it. Their intellectual life is strangely barren. And no wonder! For in common work humanity was evolved, and purely as the result of such work the human brain was developed, *and furnished with new chambers!* How then can we say that those who still engage in it are *the* un-educated. Ignorant some of them may be, and degraded even by the later forms of toil; but they are still near the source of education, since they have never ceased to work for the necessaries of life.

The schools, then, are not alien places to them— that is to say if the education given there is worth anything. For in its earlier stages education should recall earlier forms of work. But when the stage of later forms is reached the children should not be with-drawn hastily as they are withdrawn to-day. They should be allowed fearlessly and eagerly to follow the path of human progress. That is to say, they should be allowed to grow up. They must become masters of the new tools, or be mastered by them. There is no other alternative.

Until this is done there can be no lasting social

peace.   In vain the masses will ask for possession of
the means of production.   The *power of producing*
is the factor in the problem of economic life which
decides the fate of individuals and of classes.   But
the new education would offer the highest order of producing power to all who were able to win it.   And in
doing this it would not condemn all to one order of
employment, but rather give life and meaning to all
kinds of labour, and art, and learning.   It would
make clear how all these were made possible, and
the need for them created in the first place, by
work ; how every kind of learning has its origin
and source in the expanding life of a human
being struggling for food, for clothing, and shelter,
but struggling in such wise that at last he must
unlock all the secrets of Nature, use her terrible
forces for his own ends, and enter into close relations
with all his fellows.   All this will become plain
to the masses when they cease to halt, as they halt
to-day, in so far as their children are concerned, at
the threshold of the modern world—hurrying their
children of thirteen or fourteen into mills and into
casual labour as if they feared to let them fairly
escape out of the shadow of the Dark Ages.

Meantime they have to face the fact that their
children are in many cases ill, and if not ailing

themselves, are exposed every day to the risk of contact with disease and impurity. The new education discounts the results, however favourable on paper, of a system that ignores this. It recognizes that the creative power is *within* that gave us all we possess—that it reveals itself in the healthy, the growing, the vigorous, in whom the upward movement of life is not checked. In short, the new education is physiological.

.   .   .   .   .   .

The school doctor is free to take a limited view of his own functions. Even then they must appear to him to have a great social significance. Even if he does no more than condemn insanitary buildings, and insist on the prompt treatment of simple ailments, he must feel that this is something—that it is a *great* thing.

But among the ranks of members of the new profession there must be some whose thoughts will take a wider range.

These may think, perhaps, of the children of the rich *as well* as of the children of the poor. To-day the papers are filled with details of the family history and physique of a millionaire homicide. A learned counsel has read nearly every book on the physiology of the nerves, and, armed with it, now carries on a public tournament with insanity experts in the court. This display of knowledge dazzles the public, and the persons who are the subjects of his psychological dissection suffer none the less because they are placed high in the social world. They are glad to pay for " dissection " because this may save the life of an erring son and brother ? But would not the experts have done better work had they been engaged as co-operators with teachers and parents twenty years ago, and long before any crime was committed ? Truly the rich, as well as the poor, have some reason to desire the advent of the school doctor.

"But they can engage him," some may cry, "to work in a very exclusive way in the exclusive school!" No, that is impossible. There is, as we have said already, no training college here, or even in Germany, for school doctors! They have to learn by observation, and the few and comparatively small schools of the richer class do not offer a wide enough field. Not through these could they develop an entirely new branch of applied physiology —that is to say, the science of the higher brain centres and their activity and development in childhood. No; *this* work must go on where it has begun—in the people's schools. Therefore the classes, as well as the masses, have an interest in the new education.

And in the people's schools it must now go on as fast as the people will allow. Here the old garments of medievalism will be rent, its austere method exposed, its codes of punishment and torture scattered to the winds.

The new education will have none of these. It is, indeed, more personal; but it is more reverent and more gentle than the old. At every step it cautions us. We hear its voice even in the stiff German circulars. Rudeness will wreck all. The human body is not vile. It is the instrument of instruments. The first condition of success is not that the doctor has many degrees, it is that he should not offend one of these little ones. The behaviour of children—that is not a thing to judge in the first place. It is a thing to understand in the first place. To judge is easy—it has been done for ages—to understand is the new task, begun very late.[1] To

---

[1] That the German school authorities strive to get the parents to study character and temperament with the doctor and teacher is shown very clearly in some of the question-papers sent to them. For example, Dresden doctors send the following list : "Has the child had serious illnesses? Operation? Does he sleep well and quietly? Does he sleep with open mouth? Is he gay? Reserved? Truthful? Is he shy? Curious?" These questions suggest to parents the fact that faults are often symptoms—that behaviour itself is the result of physical conditions.

classify according to health is comparatively easy—it may be done by the three-card system. To classify ability and weakness is not so easy. Each child presents his own problem. In short, the class room of to-day is not the class room of yesterday. It is full of new light—and of new shadows. As time goes on, some will make strange discoveries. And some, for the sake of comfort, may pull down the blinds.

But the brave will not pull down the blinds. They will go on fearlessly to note conditions—to unearth the causes of defect, disease, suffering, and failure, to set these open to the sunshine of an enlightened public opinion, and to lay the foundations of a happier order of social life, and a new era of human progress.

FINIS

PLYMOUTH
WILLIAM BRENDON AND SON, LTD., PRINTERS

For EU product safety concerns, contact us at Calle de José Abascal, 56–1°,
28003 Madrid, Spain or eugpsr@cambridge.org.